POLITICAL CHAOS

CHAOS

Creation Of Disaster

By D.L.Bailey

 FriesenPress

One Printers Way
Altona, MB R0G 0B0
Canada

www.friesenpress.com

ISBN
978-1-03-919445-8 (Hardcover)
978-1-03-919444-1 (Paperback)
978-1-03-919446-5 (eBook)

1. POLITICAL SCIENCE, COMMENTARY & OPINION

Distributed to the trade by The Ingram Book Company

To Almighty God, and Jesus Christ our Saviour,

To my wife Elyse,

To my sons Tsion, and Canaan,

To my mother Sarah,

To my father Ron who we lost but shall be united with again!!!!!!

To my nephew Blaine,

To those brave men and women that protect us from those that would do us harm!!!

Chapters

Introduction

I have had a passion for politics for many years. Following both Canadian and American political figures and having developed a great appreciation for those men and women who put themselves in position to make a difference in their community. I have worked on Canadian Federal and Provincial elections, spanning over sixteen years. I have enjoyed the excitement of being part of a team working towards bettering our community. Working on campaigns brings you closer to the issues facing people in your community. Knocking on doors and sharing heartfelt moments with them creates an awareness of what policies are working and which ones are allowing some to be left behind. I have had the great fortune of working on many Leadership teams, with those men and women hoping to lead the Party to a brighter future. And the true honour of being elected to four terms as President of the Electoral District Association in my district. All those countless hours of talking to people about their concerns, and about their needs has been a great education for me. Watching how true leadership is done and what it looks like to put community first, has allowed me great insight into what we need as a game plan to successfully build the future. Passionate about politics in both Canada and the United States, I have watched closely what transpires when Republicans are in the White House and when Democrats are in the White House. Over the course of the last thirty-five years, I have witnessed a pattern of behaviours that I felt needed to be addressed by writing a second book based solely on how poorly the Democrats are doing at decision-making.

I feel the need for a book that showcases those key elements that are creating what I like to call, **Political Chaos.** How this chaos has been formulated, and what this chaos has manifested itself into. Americans are paying the highest price for the poor policies, and decisions that the Biden/Harris administration have both promised and kept. Americans are seeing the highest inflation in over 40 years, and the price of gas, and other consumer goods is skyrocketing. Political Chaos will look into the poor decisions, and policies that Biden has instated and made that will cement his Presidency as one of the worst of all time.

I will take you on a journey through the leadup to the 2020 election, the policies Biden has put in place after winning and taking the Oval Office, and the effect those policies are creating on life. The very policies that almost everyone on the Right, Republican, and Conservative faithful, said would lead us to where Biden has us today. The creation of and the elements of an environment that could only be described as chaotic. Rewards for the most ill behaved, ignorance of common sense, and the giving of endless money to very partisan groups. Political Chaos will highlight and enlighten readers on what the Democrat Party is allowing America to become under their watch. It has surely changed from when I first became involved in politics, and I am shocked with where we are.

Of course, my views are mine, and you the reader are of course entitled to your own, I am merely giving you an option of reading an information packed book that showcases why I can not support the Biden/Harris administration. You the reader must decide for yourselves if my opinion resounds with you, and if it makes a good argument. Having a difference of opinion is what makes life fun, debating those differences is the best environment for growth, and learning for either side.

I hope to create a compelling read for both political sides and for those that have no affiliation to any political party at all. My hope is that my books both Political Chaos and Decency and Deception will be a source of not only information and truth, but entertainment and learning. I have left humour and joking out of the writing on purpose to give full weight to the seriousness of the topic but hope to have written in such a format that would mimic a conversation.

I hope you enjoy the read; I hope to inform and counter the lack of information that currently is present in our reporting. Disagreeing with me is fine and encouraged, having your own informed opinion is essential, but it must be properly informed. What is properly informed you might ask? Well, it's contained in this book, referencing and researching your own opinion is when you will be there too. Come along with me on this journey and find out what Political Chaos looks like!!!!!!

Chapter One –

Defining Chaos

There are many contributing factors that go into the creation of chaos, like any good recipe, you need the right amounts for it to be perfect. So, creating Political Chaos takes a recipe as well, and you need a certain amount of ingredients, and we have witnessed the Democrats creating this recently. To start listing the events like ingredients would be easy enough to do, but then defining each one would take a book per event/ingredient. I will try to condense the factors and events I feel have had the most damning effect on America, and the world, for that matter. Under the leadership of Joe Biden and his Democrat side, America has projected a very weak stance to the world, and it has also gone directly against those things Americans were told to be the Biden/Harris election promises. Now before anyone says to themselves, "what politician keeps their promises", the Trump administration, despite the multiple attempts from the Left to sink them, accomplished a tremendous amount in four years. Now you can attribute those successes to Trump himself or his administration, the bottom line is, they were accomplished. Lowest unemployment, great economy, border security, job creation, etc. After his presidency, Obama tried his absolute best to claim Trump administration wins as his own, but we see since Biden has taken office, and gone back to Obama policies, that this could not be further from the truth.

So, lets break down what the definition of each word means first.

Political – relating to the government or the public affairs of a country.

Chaos - complete disorder and confusion

So, if you are talking about Political Chaos, one could relate the two definitions together to have,

Political Chaos - complete disorder and confusion involving the affairs of a country/government.

If we look at what is happening and transpiring on the Biden/Harris watch, we see that this definition defines their administration to a tee. So now we must look at the contributing factors to how we arrived in a state of Political Chaos, and what can be done to reverse course, so we can avoid the inevitable. The inevitable being complete and udder collapse of the country, and the order of law. I have identified about twenty-one factors that I feel have the biggest impact on how a Presidential administration can be a success or failure. I will outline and define each of these factors and describe how each factor is indeed important.

We will be looking at International Policy of the administration, and its impact on both America, and the world. How these policies correlate to the image presented to the world, of how competent the administration is, and how does the world view America in return. You could not present an image to the world and not have an image being presented nationally as well. We will talk about how a strong or weak image being presented to America is important. One of the most important topics of debate is energy, and the transitioning towards green energy specifically, and the best possible way of achieving that endeavor. Directly associated to green energy is infrastructure, and how building new infrastructure towards green production, like steel mills converting to electric arch furnaces will help achieve those goals and reduce our carbon footprint and emissions.

We will also look at social policy and how many in society are embracing the Defund the Police mindset and how devastating it has been on the crime rates. How a weak crime stance leads to growing concerns for public safety, and severely damages chances of rehabilitation. The greatest election goal Biden set was Unity, and the bringing back of common ground. I will showcase the path the Democrats are marching down and demanding everyone to support will never bring about unity. The executive powers Biden used in the first few days of office and continuously trying to have the House and Senate pass into law will only further eradicate that hope. If we are to find unity it will have to come at the expense of radical ideologies. Biden calling the MAGA supporters the most extreme political organization in American history, is never going to amount to Republican votes. Hillary Clinton did the same when she called Republicans deplorables, it isn't sound political practice.

The single greatest advantage a political party has at its disposal today is a powerful social media presence, with support from mainstream media, this becomes crucial during election cycles. This advantage has been very evident during the Twitter ban on Donald Trump, and how people far more controversial are still allowed the use of the platform. I will be outlining how effective this platform is and how more and more people are turning to social media for news and information. The largest problem of course is the trustworthiness of this platform and how the use of fact checkers on Conservative posts, changes people's perceptions. Without a doubt, social policies are important, and support throughout America is divided between the two Parties. I will touch on how important it is to find a balance between the two to address a substantial number of these concerns. Sadly, the way in which we voice our concerns today has become troublesome. Riots and looting or attacks on Capital buildings is not the answer, history should lead us with examples of past protests still being benchmarks of decency.

There are numerous topics that can potentially make the list of what effects a country, but topping that list must be free speech, and religious freedom. If you take away the ability of a nation to voice its concerns, or to freely talk about every topic without being,

"cancelled", you are regressing not progressing. Who oversees polic-
ing free speech? Well, that is the debate itself, should it be policed,
and is there a true definition of hate speech in today's cancel culture.
I leave cancel culture out of the equation for this book, solely for the
purpose that it needs to go away, and the idea that opposing ideas
constitute hate speech is absurd. I wrote about cancel culture in my
last book, Decency and Deception, Encouragement for a Struggling
Nation, and really covered my true feelings about it. More and more
people from both sides Left and Right, are concluding that canceling
speech or careers over a mindset is wrong. Before anyone thinks that
I am in support of any type of hate speech and support the idea of
giving it a platform to grow, you would be wrong. So, how do you
confront hate speech and support free speech, you simply call hate
speech for what it is when heard and move on without giving it a
second more of your time.

Religious freedom goes hand in hand with free speech and is being
attacked heavily today by some. If there truly exists an environment
where free speech and religious freedoms are tolerated it would not
be on social media. I will highlight the shift I feel has transpired
from religious ideology to what I call religious independence. What
religious independence means and how it plays a major part in
how religion is viewed. Why are some religions viewed as controversial and why are others based loosely on the same principals not
attacked. Is there a difference small enough to allow one more grace,
or is there a difference in perception? If one religion is allowed any
kind of tolerance, then all religions are to be given the same privilege
without condemnation. What if a group of people label religious
views as hateful, are they then allowed to be rightly attacked?

One area of difference between Right and Left leaning voters will
always be military use, and the amount of funds allocated to defence
spending. Without a strong military the world is full of bullies
looking to take advantage wherever possible. Understandably, not
everyone believes this to be true, and the amount of funding it takes
to sustain a powerful military force is staggering. The money could

be used for other policy stances like social policies, but I feel this debate will never find a mutual conclusion. I will list my stance on military power, and how effectively it changes those countries wanting to take advantage of weak leadership. I will also highlight the importance of a strong working relationship with Israel, one of the biggest Allies the West has in the Middle East.

The largest advantage a President can have is the control of both House and Senate during their term in office. I will list and mention the advantages of this support, and how it can be powerful. What activities the House and Senate work on can truly be of utmost importance to the President but can also grab the attention of the American voter. During Donald Trump's term in office the House openly worked on multiple avenues to remove him from office, teamed with mainstream media, and social media it became the largest talking point of any Presidency since Richard Nixon and Watergate. Which ironically one powerful Democrat was involved heavily in both incidents. Photo ops at the border, coining phrases like, "kids in cages" then relating overflow facilities to Nazis war camps for maximum negative imagery is appalling.

The events of the day, and the way that those events are addressed truly define Presidencies. The President is but only one aspect of the entire picture when it comes to how the Party will be viewed. Political Chaos is the absence of good decision making and is a shared blame among those in power. How those members of the House, Senate, and White House act when in power and when they are trying to gain power is crucial to image. If a subject is of utmost importance before obtaining power, like the border immigration numbers, it should be of the same importance while in power. We have come to see that this is not the case with the Biden/Harris administration or the Democrats in the House and Senate. I will address voter rights, and the Democrats wanting to allow noncitizens the ability to vote.

So many aspects ultimately influence how chaotic a Presidential term can become. The list of aspects I have chosen for this book is in direct relation to having written my first book on what has had the greatest effect on society, and I feel this book is a continuation of those concerns. Now I admit there is going to be a small amount of overlap to this book and the last, but I have tried to keep it to a minimum. Some of the topics that effect Presidents also effect the everyday American, on a daily level as well, and I wanted to create a more isolated area of critique. Like in Decency and Deception, where I isolated a timeframe in American history, I want to isolate an effect caused by decision making, policy, and the level of accountability a Presidential administration and it's President have on daily life. I want to set out the cause and effect of Joe Biden's Presidency in what has been the first year and a half. The amount of poor decision making and utter lack of interest to keep his election promises should be of great concern to Americans. The lawlessness in the streets, the crime rate, the violence, and occurrence of repeat offenders being released because bail is somehow not acceptable is appalling. The level of inflation gripping America, the shortages of food and other goods on the shelves, and the almost completely open southern border are more examples of chaos from the Biden/Harris team.

As I set out to write this book and list what I feel to be the main factors to be the creation of Political Chaos, I had to first select this subject from many very troubling behaviours I see present in today's Democratic Party platform. I ultimately went with Political Chaos because it is an entirely created state of events, and one that was specifically chosen by the Democrats. If the chaos was by chance a by-product of random acts, it would be more tolerant I feel. This leads me to why I chose the subject, I chose Political Chaos because it was completely preventable, and was something Americans were warned would happen if Biden won the election. Now I'm not saying Donald Trump is a fortune teller, or that he has any ability to see into the future, but the Republican Party did point out the border crisis, the inflation crisis, the immigration crisis, the unemployment crisis, and they plainly explained it to voters before the 2020 election took place. This book is not a Trump support and an anti-Biden talking point of any political organization. I have made these observations myself and have taken many hours of careful review, and hours of observing the actions of both sides of the story. And I am appalled at the state of things under this administration, and the people responsible should be called on their performance by those in the political world.

The one thing that Political Chaos will point out is the difference sound policy and actions have over those of poor policy and actions. We have returned to Obama style politics, with all the same results Obama had. The success Trump achieved during his term in office was a direct result of simply reversing many decisions Obama made. Trump supported Israel's capital being Jerusalem, and moved the embassy there, he reversed Iran nuke deal, health care costs came down, insulin costs specifically came down significantly. So too will the next Republican President be afforded the same advantage following Biden's Presidency and will also have great success. The argument that Obama was at all responsible for Trump's successes has officially been laid to rest I feel after Biden has brought Barack's policies back to life, with the same disadvantages being put on everyday Americans.

Political Chaos will clearly point out what decisions and party platforms have caused the country to become even more divided than when Biden took office. I will point out the reasons the Democrats are focused on things like Elon Musk taking over Twitter, and how this is concerning to them but not Jeff Bezos taking over the Washington Post, which was celebrated. Why is a business deal celebrated on one hand but enraging to the Left on the other. The chaotic state is not just isolated to the political element, education is also something very much in a state of chaos, and the ones suffering the most there are the children. Often the children are being used as political pawns, and they should be allowed to just be children, you only get one childhood, it should be something cherished. There seems to be a push from the Left to over sexualize our children, to push material on them, and to place books with graphic imagery in schools that have no business being printed let alone in schools.

And I will point out the new direction some Democrat Governors are taking to destroy future opportunities those children will be unqualified to apply to.

One aspect of the making of Political Chaos I will only briefly mention is Hollywood. I feel that the support the Democrats get from the Hollywood elite, and from daytime shows like The View, or Ellen really doesn't have much effect on people like they used to. People are starting to realize that the elite are so far removed from reality that it becomes laughable. When you are upset your vacation is put on hold because a war has broke out, lives are being destroyed, innocent people killed, but you can't go sun yourself you have lost touch with reality. So, does Hollywood matter? Award shows are starting to look more like the WWE wrestling entertainment, and the performances should have warning labels on them to prevent children from watching obscenities. Again, children being inundated with too much sexuality. However, there is still a need for movies, shows, award shows, and the likes. People enjoy going to the movies still, the fun, and excitement of a great show is something that never gets old. Politics will always have a part I feel in script writing, and rightly so, but the alienating of Conservative actors/actresses should be addressed. Ronald Reagan once upon a time, challenged Communism in Hollywood, and if only one side is allowed to be open about their politics and still work, but the other is not, we have gone back to Communist like behaviour.

The passion to which people believe their convictions is admirable, but when others feel that their stance is the only view allowed, we become subject to Marxist like social behaviours. Why is hearing opposing ideas so catastrophic to those on the Left, why must we all agree on everything? The art of debate has been lost, and the passion people used to put into the art of conversating the facts supporting those views, has been exterminated as well. The often heard saying, "I don't believe in your facts", showcases a slip in realistic reasoning. The facts are non bias, they are simply just the facts of the scenario. Emotions take president over the facts, like believing men can be pregnant, I draw the line at make belief as adults. Facts are what cement our beliefs in things, what make our resolve so staunch, and what we use to convey to others our reason for those beliefs.

You might ask yourself at the end of this book many questions about how we arrived at a state of Political Chaos if the factors are so clear. Well, misinformation and those responsible for misleading the nation, and world for that matter is a great starting point. I will point out how misinformation, silencing critics, and who might gain the most from its use. Every political campaign has some twisting or stretching of the truth, but it has never been as rampant as it is today. A great example from the past would be when Ronald Reagan ran for President against Walter Mondale in 1984. During the debate Reagan was asked a question about his age, and it being a hinderance to his ability to perform long hours like JFK did during the Cuban missile conflict. This was well played to pump Mondale up, by showcasing a win for the Democrat Party in the aversion from conflict and connect him to the very popular JFK. The efforts were quickly put to rest by Reagan's quick wit, and his ability to see the game being played before him. His answer would be one that is still talked about whenever people mention moments during debate that one side gets clear wins. Reagan simply turned the tables on Mondale, and showcased his lack of experience and youth, making them look like weakness instead of strengths. The look on Mondale's face is laughter at first, but then quickly the realization sets in that he has lost the debate, and any real chance of gaining support from the debate itself. Reagan would go on to win the election with 538 members of the Electoral College, 270 is all that is needed to win. This example showcases how some teams twist facts or information in an attempt to circumvent a failing campaign. I would like to note that Reagan didn't just win and turn the tables, he won 49 of 50 States.

These antics are still found in today's political game. The two and a half year long Mueller Investigation was almost the entire term of Trump's Presidency. How this was used to the Democrats advantage, and who used it best. The origins of this investigation are still being probed by special council Durham to this day. With any kind of blame being put on any person or group, the damage has already been done, Trump only had one term in office, but looks to make a return in the 2024 election maybe. A simple twist or helping hand given during a debate is a normal occurrence, being given the questions to the debate or plainly running narratives that are false is completely abhorrent. Instead of Disinformation Governance Boards being put into place to police free speech, behaviours of such nature before mentioned should face real consequences, and penalties in my opinion.

This will be an information loaded read. Each chapter will be filled with fascinating points, and events that have truly shaped this political landscape into the disaster it is today.

Chapter Two –

International Policy

In the world of International Policy, world leaders must stand firm, or they will be viewed by those around the world as weak and accommodating of tyrannical behaviour from those looking to impose themselves on others. Even with strong leaders we see tyranny tries to flex its muscles and it is usually at the expense of those unable to defend themselves. The list of tyrants is very lengthy, and it stretches all the way back to the Bible, so eradicating this behaviour is never going to be accomplished. So, the best way of combating such malevolence is to attack it head on, and to be strong in the face of those wishing to do others harm. This weak international policy could simply be the lack of calling another country on its behaviour like in Rwanda where the world was in shock, yet no country intervened to stop the killing of the Tutsi population.

Obama was weak on his international policy when it came to Syria and the civil uprising, where he drew a line in the sand, a redline so to speak, and then never held anyone to that deadline. As were the dealings with ISIS, and the killing of journalists unafraid of consequences from a President unwilling to adequately deal with the slayings. Barack Obama, I feel, wanted to forecast an image that terrorist groups, and terrorists themselves were somewhat of a past President problem, and his new administration was less willing to war over present issues. This was not the correct line of addressing the issue, and sadly, not only were lives lost in the Syrian conflict but also lives lost in Benghazi, Libya where American lives were lost even after being told of the attack.

So, ignoring rising conflicts around the globe only showcases to the tyrannical that there is a good chance there will not be anyone intervening to stop them. So, when we see the opposite when a world leader is elected to office, and the willingness to combat and aide those that can not help themselves is of utmost importance, we see how effective it can be. Ronald Reagan was inaugurated into office on January 20, 1981, and the hostages that had been held for 444 days were released by Tehran, Iran, within 11hrs. Why were the hostages released after such a lengthy time without even negotiating with the new administration? Well, the answer is clearly that Iran knew the former President Jimmy Carter, with his weak stance and lack of action had been replaced by a less accommodating President, fully willing to unleash the Devil itself to return those hostages.

International policy can be broken down into 4 objectives,

1. Protection of the United States, citizens, and Allies

2. Continued access to international resources and markets.

3. Preserve balance of power in the world

4. Protect human rights through democracy.

To understand the importance of these four objectives, you must review how a President or other world leaders perform at achieving success in each category. To say Obama protected American lives or Allies by ignoring the Benghazi attack that was forewarned would be a falsehood. So too is Joe Biden failing to protect American lives with so many Covid19 infected migrants flooding into the country on the southern border. The shear number of people that have flooded into the country. Stopping the border wall that Trump had well on its way to being built, simply put American lives at risk. Also, those lives of men, women, and children that attempt access to the United States illegally. Add to that the number of sex trafficking, and other criminals being caught at the border is staggering. Having what people view as an open door to bypass any vetting to gain access to immigration is dangerous, and plain and simply a desperate hope for votes by the Biden team.

Biden has decided to shut off any oil and gas production here at home. This has had a huge impact on the price of gas at the pump or heating of homes. I will talk about this decision from a production aspect later in the book, but for now I mention it as foreign policy. With the shutting down of production at home, Biden has decided to rely on the production from other countries, and in so doing, must pay their prices. Joe even went as far as to tell other countries to produce more to lower the cost of oil per barrel because his administrations decision was a failure. Leading to stickers of Joe Biden pointing with caption "I did that", on pumps across America.

With Russia invading Ukraine on February 24, 2022, it was a direct result of weak leadership in the White House. Russia has had a long-standing control issue with Ukraine and has tried many times to invade them. Back in 2014 when Joe Biden was the Vice President, Russia invaded part of the Ukraine and now we see a return to that hostility as Joe Biden is the President. A timeline of peace in the region was when Trump was in office, there wasn't a mention of an invasion. It is not just Russia wanting to flex its muscles, China has its eye on Taiwan, hoping to return that area to Chinese control as well. North Korea has been firing ballistic missiles into the ocean during the same timeframe as the Russian/ Ukraine war. There is a high level of tension in the entire region, and it has a lot to do with the current administration in the USA.

The Democrats policy to give Iran nuclear capabilities is also a failure to protect our Allies. Israel stands to be the target of Iran's ire and has openly been threatened with harm. So, giving Iran nuclear abilities and a lack of investigation or inspection by Americans is incredibly naïve and negligent. Trump was quick to cancel this Iran nuke deal that Obama brokered, and Biden wants to reinstate. Trump sanctioned Iran, and it was so effective that they were willing to sign a peace deal with Israel. Once Biden was the winner of the 2020 election that peace deal was no longer in Iran's plans, and it was not signed. It isn't difficult to see the stark difference in behaviour by those wanting to exert control and power in the region when the President is tolerant of that behaviour. We saw that ISIS was a force in hiding during Trump's four year run as President, waiting for the right time to resurrect itself.

That resurrection came when the withdrawal from Afghanistan by American troops left behind countless Allies and Americans without military support. The Taliban saw an opportunity and capitalized on it by storming the country and taking control of it. Joe Biden had to send troops back just to gain some control of the airport that was flooded with people looking for any possible way out of the region. The Afghanistan withdrawal was agreed upon by both sides, but not in the faction Biden decided to do it. Biden stated that the country would not fall fast, and that it wouldn't be like the past where helicopters had to airlift people off the roof of the Embassy. Well, he was wrong on both those statements, and lives were lost, including 13 servicemen/women doing their job for the safety of others. Those lives lost were 100 percent avoidable, and my heart breaks for each and every one.

While the actual number of military items that were left behind is not really agreed upon by many, the truth is billions of dollars worth of items were left to the Taliban in the botched withdrawal. This equipment might have been earmarked to stay with the Afghanistan forces set to take over as American soldiers withdrew. The decision to withdraw in the fashion that the Democrats chose erased any hope of recovering that equipment if they wanted to. This solidifies my earlier statement that tyrants are emboldened with weak leadership.

You could not mention countries that take advantage of a weak leader and not mention China. China has had a long history with the Biden family, both Joe and his son Hunter have spent plenty of time in the country and have dealings with Chinese businesses. I still feel that if you are in power you should not be able to, or your family should not be able to make deals with foreign companies until out of office. There is no reason that Nancy Pelosi, or Joe Biden's sons should have sat on Burisma's board of directors making a very large wage. Now you might say there is nothing wrong with setting your family or friends up with connections, but I say it should be considered an ethics violation. The Chinese have recently been accused of human rights violations with its Uyghurs ethnic group, and genocide. The 2022 Olympic games should have been boycotted or cancelled until this was investigated. Nancy Pelosi even issued a warning to American athletes to keep quiet about violations while there for their safety. That statement alone gives all authority to the Chinese to continue their behaviour, without condemnation.

Now when Trump started his Presidency many people supportive of the Left were fearful of Donald having his finger on the nuke button. This must have started out as a joke, but many people were using it as argument. Trump could not have proved them more wrong with his strong stance on peace. He had a somewhat decent report with North Korea's, Kim Jong-un, even embarking on a visit there. There was also the peace deal with the United Arab Emirates and Israel and others that should have gotten a Nobel Peace Prize nomination I feel. Trump showcased great skill at negotiations along side a firm resolve to persuade others to consider peaceful means. Russia was also respectful of Trump and his resolve, and before anyone mentions the Mueller Report or Russian collusion allegations, Hillary Clinton was more accommodating towards the Russians helping the sale of the Uranium One mining company.

Now one international or foreign policy stance that both Left and Right agree on, is aid. No matter the President the belief that the United States has some obligation to helping others is admirable. No one side can claim superiority over this area, and I think that is what sets North America apart from the rest of the world. Both Canada and the USA give graciously to those in need, not saying other countries like the UK or Germany don't give as well, only stating that I am very proud of Canada's contributions. Sometimes things differ between Democrat and Republican packages, and those items would take an entire book to list and to explain. I will just say that the differing items tend to be those same issues debated between the two sides in the United States as well. To list the difference in aid spending between Trump and Biden or Trump and Obama would be a staggering number of pages. Statistics is probably the most manipulable thing used in politics and comparing would be refuted by both sides if I were to list points. Instead, I will simply mention that both sides are gracious in their giving and leave the subject to debate by those more informed of the individual costs. Military aid is also something given, and I will cover that more in detail later in the book, but Biden's leaving billions of equipment to the Afghanistan Taliban forces was not aid, it was a disaster of immense proportions.

International trade or access to foreign markets is also a victory for both Parties. Donald Trump imposed a series of tariffs and utilized this to get tyrannical leaders to take notice. Iran, China, Mexico and even Canada were on the list. Now Canada was not a tyrannical leader, but Justin Trudeau and Trump did not have the best relationship. The North American Free Trade deal was updated under Trumps administration to the USMCA, and it showcased Trump's desire to strengthen the advantages that could be found. Having strong trade relations sets the countries apart that face sanctions and poorly negotiated deals. Countries like the Hamas led Palestinian West Bank suffer under sanctions, but it is the best way to limit the access to war materials. Sadly, not all countries have democratic freedoms, and elections and accountabilities are not afforded to them.

Speaking of freedoms, during the Covid19 early breakout, we witnessed Trump place a travel ban in March of 2019. This was met with furious vigor from those on the Left, and even Biden mocked it as Covid19 is an airborne disease. Pelosi insisted people get out and do things, as did countless others from the Left. Mayor Del Blasio insisted people ride the subway and other activities. But after this insistence when numbers effected was staggering, wanted to place all blame on Trump squarely, with no ownership of having persuaded the public to callously take less precautions. Trump also placed bans on certain countries due to those being hotbeds for terrorist activities. Now you would think this would have been celebrated by everyone as a safety precaution, making American lives more protected. Well, you would be wrong because it was used to further promote a xenophobic image being presented by the Left of Donald Trump. The same bans would be later used by Joe Biden but when asked about those same bans, then White House Press Secretary, Jen Psaki would say that Trump banned the people, but Biden is banning the country. This blatant, childish behaviour is what needs to be further called out and pushed back upon until no one wants to be embarrassed by such brutally unethical behaviour. Yes, unethical behaviour because it attempts to destroy a person not the policy of an administration but the very character of the person, and it is wrong on all levels. Travel bans of countries or a ban on the people behaving in such manners that endanger others lives and wellbeing is important, and necessary.

When it comes to supporting our Allies, Trump made a very grand gesture by moving the American Embassy to Jerusalem, the capital of Israel. The battle between Israel and the Palestinians is not going away anytime soon, and Israel has long been our greatest friend and Ally in the region which means we should support their claim to Jerusalem as its capital. Not to say that the Palestinian side has no support from America, President Jimmy Carter stands firmly with Palestine as does Rashida Tlaib and others. Jerusalem being claimed as capital by both sides and any desire to split the city would be very difficult. I pray for a peaceful resolve and hope for less tensions.

During Obama's time as President, we witnessed an agreement with Iran who are very vocal in their wishes for the state of Israel. Once that nuclear deal with Iran was signed, Israel had major concerns about the safety of their country from attacks. Obama at one point was considering stopping the shipment of munitions to Israel over their building new homes and apartments in areas of concern for

Palestinian leaders. This did little to strengthen relations between Obama and Netanyahu, but concerns were voiced, speeches given, and in the end, Bibi was left to await a new President. Enter Donald Trump, and he reached out to Netanyahu only days after his inauguration. The canceling of the Iran nuke deal also was of favour to both men, and Israeli defense munitions for their Iron Dome were solidly backed by Trump.

Democrat Eric Swalwell from California's 15th district found himself in trouble when he allowed Christine Fang, or Fang Fang, a Chinese spy close access to his office. It is believed she was not successful in gaining any information, but for Swalwell to be on the Intelligence committee, and allow this kind of access to anyone is shamefully naïve. Eric was very active in investigating Trump and the Russian collusion theory, and I find it humorous that his efforts to remove Trump from office ended up with Swalwell being involved with foreign spies himself, and Trump found to not have colluded with the Russians. This should have not been a vote issue, to which Swalwell survived by a vote 218-200-3 to remain on the Intelligence committee, it clearly showcases a lack of judgement on Swalwell's behalf and a concern for national security. Swalwell should have been removed, and the fact he was not, is problematic.

During the end of Trump's administration, it is reported that General Mark Milley made phone calls to China, secretly behind Trump's back. Now, of course removing a top General would look very poorly for the United States, and would lead to some disciplinary hearings, I'm sure. Many are spinning this to make Milley look like he saved WWIII from happening, and that China was about to escalate tensions or something of that manner. The truth is, General Milley should have went to his President first and asked for the role or spoken with at least Vice President Pence. Choosing to trust the Chinese over your own country, should have removed you from office. Now, given that I was not present for the calls I shouldn't automatically assume the worst, but I feel it was the wrong decision, that's just my opinion of course. Defending your actions after an undertaking of this manner doesn't change the actions taken. Milley continues to hold his post, only being held accountable in the court of public opinion.

Presidents' foreign policies have long been subject of debate and remains one of the most important aspects of any administration. The well being of the economy and the stability of the dollar are all linked to it. One of the most important aspects of strong foreign/international policy is image, the view the rest of the world has on the President and his/her advisors. As pointed out, having a strong stance is crucial to keeping a better hold on the conflicts around the globe. This is just one of many failures we see of the Biden Presidency. The Taliban, Russia, China, and North Koreans all taking full advantage of weak leadership. The southern border being overrun with immigrants and the flooding of the very facility that the Democrats called, "kids in cages", and "concentration camp", under Trump. Biden's image abroad is not of strong leadership, and we all know that image is very important.

Chapter Three –

International Image

Like I mentioned already in the last chapter, the image projected to the malevolent leaders around the world, is a very important tool to the President of the United States of America. The image the world has of a President's abilities to perform the job, and to be someone worth aligning themselves with is key to the success of their term in office. Now, over the years we have had many different men hold the office of the President of the United States, and no one Party can claim they are without conflict. Those conflicts, and how they were handled are what sets the two-Party leaders apart.

Let's first start with George W. Bush, and the attacks on 9/11. The terrorists decided to plan and carry out these attacks on the Pentagon, World Trade Towers, and what could have been the White House or Capital Building. Some have suggested that the original intent was to carry out the attacks while Clinton was in office. And the result would have gone without push back as Democrats would be less likely to use military force. I am not sure if Osama Bin Laden thought the attack would generate a war, or if he was hoping for one, but war was what he got. The entire area around Iran, Iraq, Syria, Afghanistan, and Pakistan was a hotbed of tensions, and Bush put America in the battle to push back for the 9/11 attacks. Whether there were any weapons of mass destruction or not, America was there to punish those responsible for the lives lost. Bush was projecting an image of strength to those wishing harm on America, and he was not going to sit by and take it. He took advantage of being in the region, and went after Iraq dictator Saddam Hussein, who also was very malevolent in his use of power. Bush stated Saddam would face justice, having denied millions that same privilege. And on December 14, 2003, Bush announced Saddam Hussein had been captured. This projected a very positive image for Bush and allowed the world the opportunity to witness accountability for actions. Hussein would face a trial and be found guilty of crimes against humanity, willful killing, illegal imprisonment, deportation, and torture, and was sentenced to death by hanging.

This capturing, and removal of such a powerful leader I feel is what gave empowerment to those freedom fighters wanting to have the same for their country in Libya. With the capture and killing of Muammar Muhammed Abu Minyar al-Gaddafi, the world was starting to stand up to leaders wishing to supress them. It was a direct result of the image being projected, that enough was enough, and time had run out on tyrannical leadership. Bush may not have been in power when Osama Bin Laden was killed, but he was directly responsible for the changing of the guard in that region, and the empowerment given to the people wanting to come out from under the boot of suppression.

After George Bush we had Barrack Obama, and the escalation of terrorist activities in Syria, and Iraq. Obama once called ISIS, JV, meaning they were really a low threat, or juvenile. That description would come back to haunt him, as ISIS would become a very imposing power in the region, with countless lives being affected by their actions. Obama would not gain the upper hand on the situation and would eventually try what was effective for the Bush administration and go capture and kill Osama Bin Laden. It would not have the same result for the Obama administration, as he had already projected a weak image of being tolerant of many timelines coming and going in the Syrian conflict. A case of too little too late, the world had already witnessed Obama fail to save journalists being beheaded and others dying in very painful and inhuman ways, all being video taped and played for the world. People were leaving their countries to join ISIS from all over the world, and fight along side these terrorists. The shear empowerment given to these terrorists, and without accountability was infuriating. The malevolent just didn't see the Obama administration as a threat to their behaviour and were acting as if the parents had left the children at home for the weekend, then enter Donald Trump to the office of the Presidency.

With Trump taking over for Barack Obama the shift of power went from weak leadership to an image of powerful leadership. ISIS, Taliban, and Al-Qaeda all went into a quiet phase, where they didn't carry out many attacks and were very low key. This is not to say it wasn't a period of planning on their part, or that they had gone away. Leaders of these terrorist groups were being the target of drone strikes, and airstrips were bombed keeping air traffic to a minimum. The image Trump and his team put forward was effective enough to keep those usual characters at bay, and work diligently on peace in many areas of the world. This was one of the biggest successes of Trump's term in office. Once being portrayed by the Democrats and Left faithful as the potential reason for WWIII, Trump was nominated for the Nobel Peace Prize, and if given a second term would have received it, I feel. The greatest by-product of having a positive or strong image for a President is the ability to use that image to broker peace. This is probably the biggest reason the Democrats didn't target any of the Trump administration successes, but rather focused solely on Donald J Trump himself. His policies were making historic gains, and the Democrats could not argue differently. If they could destroy the man responsible for those successes, well then, they could hope to erase, or lessen those historic gains. Portraying Trump as a traitor, cheat, tax cheat, woman hater, racist, power abusing, and who knows what else was effective as there are people that argue these points as the truth to this day. Proof being the spoiler of the debate, but because it was portrayed by the media so enthusiastically, and often, people believe it, even without proof.

Russia invading Ukraine twice under Joe Biden being in power is no coincidence. Obama and Biden share an image that differs from that of Donald Trump. During Trump's term in office Russia didn't invade but when Joe Biden was vice president and president, Russia felt as if they could. Vladimir Putin used the weak stance on war, and the weak image Joe Biden was projecting as a frail, cognitively declined leader to his advantage. Biden's cognitive decline is discussed more in the next chapter, but I want to just mention his cognitive abilities, and many gaffs on live coverage have not helped his image any. This conflict is ongoing well into Biden's second year as President, and countless lives have been lost. But it isn't just Russia that is pushing the limits, North Korea has been testing rockets towards the sea often, and without any real attention from the White House. China has been making gestures of wanting to invade Taiwan and return them to China's control. So why would these countries threaten such chaotic behaviour? Well, it views the US as less of a threat to use military pressure to regain normal interactions.

Policies that leaders place into action, or the stances that are taken on key issues around the world are important factors to president's having a positive image. I feel that Biden has hurt himself with the Afghanistan pullout, and with an overall image of willingness to work with countries that don't treat their people well, like China. Biden has had years of interaction with Xi Jinping, China's leader, even though there have been accusations of human rights violations. If Biden was unwilling to call the treatment of the Uyghurs by the Chinese government, a potential genocide, he looks to be tolerant of their treatment. Other policies like support for NATO and commitments like the Paris Accords, have helped his image. Trump pulled out of the Paris Accords due to the amount of money and little effect the States had on the climate compared to China, who continues to not change climate/emissions levels.

The Paris Accords is an agreement between 196 parties, on climate change, mitigation, adaptation, and finance. Climate change has been and continues to be a very important driving factor for a successful future. Biden's commitments to climate change at home is a point I will write about in this book, however, Biden's reliability on other countries to produce oil and gas for the dependency of the United States is hypocritical. If you have a dependency on fossil fuels and choose to cancel any extraction of those fuels nationally, but want other countries to feed, over produce for costs, and ultimately, accrue those emission credits so you don't have to, is very irresponsible, and noncommittal to your own beliefs. It contributes to your image looking weak and hypocritical.

With a lowered international image, the Party will have a hard time aligning itself with that individual to have continued success in their local ridings. As the view or image, the leader has, it will ultimately reflect negatively, or positively upon those working along side that leader. In the instance the leaders image suffers, fellow candidates will have to distance themselves from them while elections are taking place, and where otherwise the leader would campaign with those running for House, Senate, and Governor positions, a poor image would be more of a hindrance than help. This was the case for Biden during the 2022 Midterm elections, where Obama was called upon to campaign for many instead of Joe.

Leaders from other countries that want to either gain popularity at home or upgrade their image internationally will do the same, distance themselves from those that will hinder those chances. Image can change quickly as then Israeli Prime Minister Naftali Bennett went from laughing at Biden during their first visit at the White House when Biden became confused, to working to strengthen ties between the two countries. Israel needs the Allied support of the United States as they are often in conflict with Hamas and needing supplies to protect themselves using their Iron Dome defense system.

During Jimmy Carter's Presidency, 52 United States diplomats and citizens were held hostage for 444 days. On November 4, 1979, hostages were held after a group of militarized Iranian college students belonging to the Muslim Student Followers of the Imam's Line, in support of the Iranian Revolution, took over the Embassy in Tehran. Regardless of what led to the hostage situation, the subsequent failure on behalf of Jimmy Carter to negotiate, and free those hostages, led to his defeat to Ronald Reagan in the 1980 election. His image was tarnished to the point that he only carried 6 States plus DC, a very handed defeat. Ronald Reagan ran on many campaign promises, one being that if those hostages were not released within 12 hours of his inauguration, military action would be swift. They were released to American support at 11 hours of his inauguration. Carter's image of being weak, along with the failed military effort cost him much more than the office of President, it put his name at the top of the list of worst President's. I would like to say that Jimmy Carter may not be a favourite President of mine, but I admire the man he is, and the family first Christian that he has steadfast been. His image as leader maybe lacking, but his character, humanity, and spirit are without a doubt impeccable. Jimmy Carter is a good man.

Ronald Reagan took over the office of President January 20, 1981, and within hours the hostage situation that had lasted 444 days was over. His threats of elevated military action and wiliness to use that power, were taken literally by the hostage takers, and wisely so. Reagan would put forward a strong image his entire Presidency. This strong image is what the Democrats would tarnish with the use of media, television shows, and celebrities. He would be made to sound and act only interested in jellybeans instead of what President's should be focused on. Again, tarnish the man, erase his achieve-ments. Winning the Cold War against the Russians wasn't accom-plished with low intelligence, but rather speaks to Reagan's genius. During the Cold War Reagan and Mikhail Gorbachev would form a friendship, and albeit a political friendship, but one that could be useful to quell tensions between two countries. For years the threat of war with Russia was present. Dating all the way back to WWII when Patton said Russia would only be trouble in the future. John F. Kennedy would have one of his greatest moments with the Cuban Missile Crisis, and Russian missiles headed for Cuba. Reagan would eventually quiet this chaos with diplomacy, and strength of character. Reagan telling Gorbachev to, "tear down this wall", will be a moment forever aligned with strong leadership.

Ronald Reagan would continue to build his great image through many situations. The greatest I feel is his assassination attempt at the hands of John Hinckley Jr. on March 30, 1981, where he was shot and wounded. Reagan was rushed to hospital at first unaware of the extent of his injuries, only to find out he had broken a rib, punctured a lung, caused serious internal bleeding. He was, near death when he arrived at hospital. Other men were also wounded on this day, Michael Deaver, Thomas Delahanty, Tim McCarthy, and James Brady, who was the most wounded of all. After the assassination attempt Reagan would use his humour to further cement his image, and during a speech in Berlin when someone popped a balloon, Reagan never missed a beat and yelled, "missed me", then continued his speech. This was met with loud cheers from the crowd, that caused the speech to pause. Reagan's jokes, humour, and ability to warm a crowd to his personality quickly, were admired by many world leaders. Canadian Prime Minister Brian Mulroney and Reagan would often be seen singing Irish songs together, and Britain's Iron Lady, Margret Thatcher would share a fondness so evidently strong that at his funeral she was filled with grief. Thatcher would ask Reagan's help with her own country's problems, and with the Falkland Islands and her political name at stake, she would strike swiftly against the Argentine military junta, and elevate her image. Cementing the fact that strong leaders, will broker strong fellowship of other strong leaders.

Trump belongs in the same category as Reagan when it comes to position of military readiness. The fact ISIS was dormant during his term in office is evidence of that. Many Presidents have had a positive impact on the world, but some stand head and shoulders above them all. I feel Reagan was one of 5 Presidents that helped change the world and made a difference for the better. Abraham Lincoln would have been a man of immense fame had the times been different. Had the internet or social media been available the world would have known of his fight to better the lives of millions of Americans. I put him on the list because his image to everyone around the world is still that of greatness, and no list would be complete without him on it. My list of great Presidents is based upon their image, how the world saw them, and how they effectively changed something for the better. Barack Obama was incredibly Presidential, very personable, and charming, he had cool oozing out of his very being. Unfortunately, he had failed policies and weak military stance to wash away that cool fast. My list is not just war Presidents, but men of strength, able to create opportunity with image and hope through positivity.

Top 5 Presidents based on image and accomplishment,

1. Ronald Reagan   – Cold War
2. FDR   - World War II
3. John F. Kennedy   - Cuban Missile Conflict
4. Teddy Roosevelt   - Rough Riders
5. Abraham Lincoln   – Emancipation Proclamation

Now no list of best Presidents could be posted without the list of worst President based on image and failed opportunity. The list is comprised of men based on the same credentials but were the Presidents that left us wanting.

1. Richard Nixon - Watergate
2. Bill Clinton   - USS Cole bombing/ Monica Lewinsky
3. Jimmy Carter   - Iranian Hostages
4. Barack Obama   - Syria/ISIS
5. Joe Biden   - Afghanistan/Inflation/Border

I would like to mention some honourable names that I didn't put on my list. George Washington would have been an absolute hero today based on his leadership accomplishments. Dwight Eisenhower perhaps should have made the list based solely on his leadership of Allied Forces during the D-Day invasion. As a man that had 5 Uncles, 2 more in reserves, and my wife's grandfather who was on Juno Beach on D-Day, I feel Eisenhower deserves a place by himself for leadership. I could not be more thankful to him and the victory that saw these men come home.

There are a few names that would have made the list of poor Presidents as well. Just because I feel these men failed at creating opportunity or an image of strength, does not mean they were without some moments of accomplishment. I think we often state the negative over the positive, but in this case I do so to highlight the topic of the chapter. These 46 men have met the challenge head on and won elections to be in the position of President, which is a great accomplishment. Lyndon Johnson and the Vietnam War would have put him on the list higher if it weren't for the Obama/Biden twosome that both used the same failed policies. Obama created the policies, showcased the failure they possessed then highlighted those same failures when resurrected by the Biden Presidency. These men could potentially share a spot on the list opening a spot for LBJ. Johnson will remain engrained in conspiracy theory over the assassination of JFK, which is a very unsavory image to say the least. There has never been proof obviously of any foul play towards Johnson, but that is what conspiracy theory is all about.

The image put forward is crucial to success, and legacy is built off what others perceive of you. It works for politics, sports, acting, and everyday life. Fathers, Mothers, teachers, and friendships are all based on how we are perceived by those around us. If we put forward our best self, we project strength and leadership. If we put forward not our best self, we suffer the consequences of those actions. We in turn let our families down, our co-workers, our bosses, and most importantly ourselves. The image across the globe as President mirrors the image here at home as well. That image is of the most importance to the continuation of being President.

Chapter Four –

Weak Image Nationally

Continuing with image but switching it up to how a President is viewed at home, we see a lot of similarities for negative effects. The two images, both positive and negative, go hand in hand, both internationally and domestically, and are very much responsible for the legacy created by those terms in office. So, can a President have a poor image Globally, but be popular at home in the USA? Well, the answer is yes, because the factors could potentially be different, or the person running against them could be even worse. Hillary Clinton's image was more flawed than Donald Trump's, then add Bill Clinton's reputation to Hillary's and it was a complete disaster. Sure, Hillary was popular in the usual circles like Hollywood, and Blue States, but not enough to carry her to the office of President. Would Hillary Clinton have been a good President? I guess we will never know that answer, but she doesn't have as many positive aspects about her as she does negative, which is quite a lot. Her image as a less trustworthy candidate, and her scandal plagued leadup and campaign run didn't help her cause. Hillary would have been a far better choice for Vice President for Joe Biden, but for reasons unknown to me, Kamala Harris was given that role.

Kamala Harris is a perfect definition of poor image causing problems for future consideration. I feel if Kamala Harris was more popular than Joe Biden, she would already be President of the United States. Her ability to say nothing during speeches, and her reputation as a person that laughs off situations she can't control or answer, sink her popularity. Her popularity has continuously been lower than Joe Biden's, which is also at an all time low. Harris's reputation as a lawyer was subject to some colourful debate moments during her candidacy for the Democratic Party nomination to run against Donald Trump in 2020. I will not mention any of those comments as I have learned to not tangle with lawyers, even if there is reasonable belief. I feel Kamala Harris hurt herself by believing Joe Biden was inappropriate towards Tara Reade, being vocal in that belief, then forgetting all about his actions to run as his running mate and Vice President. Staying true to your convictions is a difficult endeavor in politics, but as a woman Harris should have either defended women's rights or remained silent on the issue. She should have declined the position if she truly felt Biden was in the wrong. By accepting the position of VP and going silent on the situation Kamala looks opportunistic, saying what she feels women wanted to hear, but then giving a free pass to Biden. Maybe the position was worth more to her.

The image put forward by would be candidates, or by Presidents hoping for re-election must be sound, and it must be one of competence. George H. W. Bush was given only one term as President due mainly to his increasing taxes, which most would agree needed to be done at the time. He also represented another four years of Republicans being in the White House, after following Ronald Reagans eight years in power. It was more timing that Bill Clinton won the White House than platform. Clinton would have eight years in power, and see a strong economy, but will forever be remembered for his potential impeachment over the Monica Lewinsky affair, or the statement he never had sexual relations with her, but then had to admit he did. If his Presidency is remembered more for the affair, he had over his actions to help the country prosper he didn't make a big enough difference. If you add the attack on the USS Cole, and the lack of making those that came forward claiming responsibility for the attack, pay for those actions, it only further erodes your legacy.

As mentioned earlier, when Ronald Reagan was running against Walter Mondale, there was a question posed to Reagan during debate about his advanced age, and ability to perform long hours. Reagan would turn this attempt around on his younger opponent and create an image of strength out of it. By changing the onus of disadvantage from being too old, to an advantage of having strength of wisdom and experiences to handle the job better. And it worked, after Reagan stated this answer both Mondale, and the American people knew Reagan had hit a homerun. The moment was met with silence to which Reagan felt compelled to fill with more points about his abilities. The moment is one of the greatest debate wins in history and led to Ronald Reagan winning all but one State in his re-election bid. I believe this is the greatest Presidential debate moment, showcasing how to best present yourself. One of the worst moments in Presidential debate history came after the debate itself, when it was revealed that Hillary Clinton had obtained the debate questions before hand and didn't notify anyone of this egregious act. This didn't help Clinton's chances of being President, it only hindered it, which is maybe the best payback for cheating.

Being able to convince the opposition to work with you and your agenda to get policy, and law passed through the House and Senate, is incredibly hard to do. Biden's Build Back Better agenda is not an example of when this has happened. Build Back Better isn't even something all Democrats can vote yes on and haven't. When you control the House and Senate you should have zero issues passing your agenda unless it is filled with flawed elements. This was the case when Joe Manchin D-West Virginia, voted no on Build Back Better and caused his own Party to pressure him to change his mind. Others were targeted in the washroom. A failure becomes much more when that failure destroys the workability of the Party as a whole. If you create inner Party chaos, then it is sure to die on the floor of the House and Senate as no opposition Party member will vote yes. It is very important to keep an open, and healthy working relationship between the two Parties, we have not seen this during Trump's Presidency or Joe Biden's. Republicans were the majority in the Senate for Trump's term in office, and thankfully so with the Democrats openly trying to remove him from office through impeachment. These failed attempts to impeach and the constant investigations put forward by Democrat led committees destroyed that fabric of unity. Biden's Presidency has witnessed inner Party bickering, and finger pointing by the four-woman group known as, "The Squad".

The main difference between Republicans and Democrats tends to be what they believe in fundamentally. What they believe is most important, needs to be defended to the core. Well, this is where Republicans tend to be more inline with each other, as opposed to the many different groups of demographics that are found under the Democrat umbrella. If you are more alike in main beliefs, and more alike in your principal platform, the chances of support are greater. If your support group is made up of many different groups, all fighting for their cause to be heard and given more attention, there is a greater chance of imploding from within before finding cohesiveness. If you have five groups that supported your run to office, and you became President, which group gets the lions share of your attention, and will the other groups approve of being second rate? The answer is quite definitely no, and time will only make matters worse as hurt feelings, and campaign promises that have not been kept fester.

Making realistic campaign promises, and attempting to keep those promises, being a person of your word, is very important to building a positive image for voters to place their trust in. Trump made some very large proclamations as his campaign promises. He said he would build a southern border wall, to protect America from the influx of illegal immigrants. It would have been fully built if he would have won a second term. The number of illegals crossing into the United States per month was nothing compared to Biden's numbers, and yet the Democrats fought against the border wall. Trump said he would return jobs that had left for good, or so Obama said. Obama also made statements about Trump having a magic wand to make GDP grow again, and in fact Trump doubled it. Trump's job creation was up 399% over Obama's last 26 month in office, now that's keeping campaign promises.

Biden made a promise to beat Covid19, stated 220,000 deaths should make you ineligible for office. Since Biden has taken office over a million have now died, does his remark still stand, or can we get a journalist to ask him to clarify. Biden promised he would beat cancer, really Joe, cancer? Well, we all know this isn't getting done anytime soon, so why use it, why no push back from media? Biden's biggest failure so far has been his promise concerning unity. Biden went from saying we will have to come together and unify the country, and he was the guy to get it done. Then decided Republicans were racists, that the MAGA supporters were the most extreme political organization in American history, or at least recent history. When Hillary called Republicans and supporters deplorables it didn't work well for her, so why is name calling being brought back by the side saying we need to be unified. Surely, they understand that name calling, and temper tantrums have no place in running the country. The real problem is the Democrat side uses division and pushes for further division. It was the Democrat side that attacked ads put forward referencing Jesus at Super Bowl LVII. The Democrats can't afford people flocking to church, building unity, because faith can truly build unity better than politics ever could.

Now Trump did make other predictions during the campaign. He said Joe Biden's policies would cause $7/per gallon gas prices, he said inflation, job loss, unemployment numbers and border crisis would be the inevitable outcome of Democrat logic. He was right, he proclaimed it then Joe Biden fulfilled it. During the next election in 2024, the chances of a more popular person coming along and highlighting these predictions and the fact they came true, are very great. Now one advantage the Biden/Harris administration has over the Republican side is the mainstream media, social media platforms, and Hollywood writers, stars and programs building up Democrat candidates where there isn't any real material or accomplishments.

Like when Whoopi Goldberg stated on The View that Jill Biden was a great doctor, that she heard Jill was great. Only to be informed she has a doctorate in education. So why build up Jill Biden and refuse any invites to Melania? I think the answer to that question might be a book all to itself.

Let's talk about the 25th Amendment and the effects it would have not just on Joe Biden, but the Democrat Party, and Kamala Harris as well. The Democrats knew before Trump's term in office was over that Biden was their candidate, and Nancy Pelosi stated that any future consideration would not be about Donald Trump, but about future use. So, the Democrats had to have an idea that Joe's age could be a potential problem. The Democrats may have used the 25th Amendment already if Kamala Harris wasn't less popular than Joe. So, what is the 25th Amendment and what does it do? Well, the 25th amendment is designed to remove power from the President if he/she becomes unable to perform their duties. It sets out four sections, and if that power can be returned or permanently removed.

Section 1   If the President is removed from office, dies, or resigns the Vice President becomes President (not acting President). Used when Richard Nixon resigned.

Section 2   If the Vice President position is vacant the President nominates someone to replace. Voted on by House and Senate to become Vice President. Gerald Ford replaced Spiro Agnew.

Section 3   President can declare themselves "unable to discharge the powers and duties of the Office". Letter sent to House and Senate, the VP becomes acting President, and a letter written to reclaim power. Reagan gave power to George H. W. Bush for medical procedure.

Section 4   Allows executive officials to declare the President unable to do his job. The Vice President must agree to do this. This portion of the amendment has not been used.

Joe Biden could become the first President to be removed from office using Section 4 of the 25th amendment, his decline and confusion has gotten worse, Kamala Harris would become the acting President.

During times when we see Republicans polling better than Democrats, Hollywood goes crazy trying to change the view Americans have on those Republicans. Attacks today are more of a personal nature the attacks are designed to make America believe the most heinous acts are supported by the people in office. Attacking a person to depict them as racist, xenophobic, misogynist, transphobic or any other label is the new thing. Labelling people under these categories is created to destroy any credibility so that people's jobs, family life, friends, party affiliation, or interests is affected. Wanting to cancel people of opposite belief, or opinion is fundamentally wrong, and it showcases a genuine lack of human empathy. We need to get back to embracing those differences, not canceling them, so we only hear what we believe and think, echo chambers are not great environments. How will we ever grow and foster better relationships if we can't challenge ourselves with provoking thoughts?

The easiest place to attack others today is on social media, and it is done without any face-to-face interactions at all. These online personas people create for themselves have become the main way people interact with others. In a time when texting, and online chat groups have taken a more superior roll than that of meeting and verbally communicating, it is becoming easier for people to be emboldened, and to attack others for just about anything. Religious ideology, or political preferences, are very volatile subjects. Gender, pronouns, and the words, "I identify as", have become the focus of many people. Jordan Peterson's rise to fame came from his unwillingness to use pronouns that have now been legislated by the Liberal Government of Justin Trudeau, to use. A first in Canadian history, that words be legislated, clear example of infringement of our Freedom of Expression. So, should we use these pronouns, and are we obligated to refer to everyone that wants to identify as something of their own choosing? The answer to that question is not easy, and it should be written in this chapter I feel because it goes towards a person's image.

If you have any enjoyment in a friendship, and that person changes their pronoun, or identifies as something new, would you not do as asked to continue in that friendship? Well, the answer is yes, and people would be more willing to accommodate this request from a close friend. Does it change if the person isn't a close friend, but rather a work acquaintance? Nothing has changed except the nature of the friendship; the request has remained the same. So, it becomes a personal choice if we follow the requested pronoun, or gender, and you will be viewed or create an image of being for or against. Now, your stance will surely be of subject matter on social media if you choose a strong stance on the issue. Choose your stance wisely, it can be a very volatile subject for some.

Moving on to how poor image can affect your interactions with Governors at the State level becoming a hinderance to your agenda as President. A President must keep a working relationship with those State Governors to ensure there is fluidity between the two levels of Government. The relationship is a two-way street, and it can be problematic at times. Florida's Ron DeSantis has battled with Joe Biden over mask mandates and Covid19 freedoms from the beginning. DeSantis removed mask mandates and opened businesses, while Democrats continued to push mask usage along with shutdowns to businesses. The problems caused by these shutdowns to the economy, and to mental health has been far reaching. The real problem is hypocrisy from the Democrats themselves as Florida was a hotbed for Democrats vacationing, all the while demanding shutdowns, and mask mandates in their

States. Alexandria Ocasio-Cortez was ridiculed for vacationing with her boyfriend, without masks, and in businesses open to the public freely. Her answer to this hypocrisy was that people were upset because they wanted to date her. While Florida, and Texas were benefiting from opposition to Biden's lockdowns, and mandates, other States were suffering greatly for following them. To have States disobeying Federal statutes and being successful in doing so looked very poorly on the Biden administration. Enter misinformation to the mix and over the course of this battle, Florida would have to correct data that was incorrect about numbers of sick people, hospitalization, and deaths. At one point the collective of all deaths was reported in error as a single day death count.

Another instance of a Governor making Biden look bad was in Texas, over the border crisis. Texas has been overrun with illegal immigrants flooding into the USA, across the southern border. Trump wanted to have this problem under control with the finalization of the wall. As Biden and Harris refuse to visit the border or border facilities where these illegals are being detained, the problem worsens. Biden's team is working on making it more accessible with policies, and incentives. At one point considering giving millions of dollars to these illegal immigrants. Up to one million dollars to couples, and five hundred thousand dollars per person. To combat this Texas Gov. Greg Abbott started using border guards on horse back and was having great success. I will cover this in more detail in the chapter Immigration.

Quite clearly image is important. It makes all the difference in the world to the success of a Presidents term in office. How the world sees the administration, and the ability to lead with confidence effects more that people realize. The stock markets, trading, development, and economies are all interlinked to image and perception. It has a powerful grip on State interaction, and voter confidence, deciding the future plans a President may have. The image Joe Biden leaves after his term in office is over will have a direct effect on the next President. If the next President is Republican, it will surely be easy enough to reverse some if not most of Biden's decisions. Will it have the same positive effect it did for Trump following Obama, we will have to wait and see. If the next President is a Democrat, a continuation of the same, and poor policies that are destroying America, future Democrats will have to answer for the failures.

Chapter Five –

Poor Energy Policy

The biggest mistake the Biden/Harris administration has made starting their term in office was to give into pressure on Green Energy. I'm all for lowering our emissions, and for finding more environmentally sound practices to improve our planets health. The planet is no different than our own bodies, it needs to be cared for properly to optimize the benefits. When we transition away from fossil fuels, we will become better for having done so. Biden within days of being inaugurated, decided to ban renewing leases on Government land for extraction of fossil fuels. Why is this bad, if we all agree we must eventually transition away from these fuel sources? The answer is simple, we are still dependant on fossil fuels, and if there is a cancellation on extraction in the United States, then we must buy it elsewhere until we have developed a new source.

One of the biggest talking points for Biden is how he has kept his promise of canceling fossil fuel production. Two main effects of this poor decision have been rocketing unemployment, and increased prices at the pump. Both negatively affect Americans, and at a time when people have faced struggles due to Covid19 shutdowns, and mandates. When people are finding it difficult to make ends meet, the last thing any administration should be working on is how to increase those difficulties. There are many areas affected by shutting down fossil fuel industries, and the greatest is to the worker. Biden has also released millions of barrels of reserve oil, stored for instances of emergency, like if war breaks out. Biden's decision to release this oil is a huge mistake, and China is buying the oil released.

Unemployment due to the cancelled extraction of gas and oil has been staggering. Biden mislead people during his run for office that those workers that would lose their jobs would be trained to work in the Green Energy field. Well, this is not a simple conversion, and to my knowledge there has been limited if any moves to build Green Energy sources. Workers in each State that becomes a potential source should already be transitioning into training, so they are ready to start once Green Energy production begins. The truth is, this process will take far longer than Biden's term in office, and years of construction to finalize. The real scary fact is that Trump said this unemployment would happen, and the affects of this poor decision. With the lack of production, but the need for oil and gas, Biden is relying on other producers around the globe for their product, Biden is also directly responsible for their workers having jobs. All at the expense of our own workers, and low price we would pay at the gas pump, heating bill, business expenses. Biden could not have made a worse decision if he wanted too.

The main reason for the cancelled oil and gas extraction is a call from withing his own Party, people like Alexandria Ocasio-Cortez, who unrealistically think this transition should be immediate, and the trillions of dollars needed, passed through the Senate and House without hesitation. It just doesn't work that way, and no matter how loudly one demands it, processes should have evaluations and esti-mates beforehand. So, to appease his own fellow Democrats, and those voters supporting Green Energy, Biden put both feet in, and virtue signalled that his administration is serious about Climate. What happened is exactly what everyone knowledgeable said would happen, and it is disappointing to say the least.

I will point out a few areas I feel are the main contributors to why this is such a devastatingly poor decision, and then describe each of the areas in more detail.

1. Dependency on Fossil Fuel

2. Cancelled Pipeline

3. Green Energy Promise

4. Investments into Green Energy

5. Coal Mining

6. Job Creation Promise

7. Buying Foreign Oil/Gas

8. Solar and Wind

9. Investment into diverse areas

10. Costs of Training Workers

11. Costs of Cleanup

12. Inflated prices to consumers

13. Carbon Footprint

Just to reiterate, with the poor decision to cancel further extraction, unemployment has skyrocketed. And at a time when Biden was making even more decisions that were causing unemployment to increase in other areas like construction, with the border wall construction cancellation. Both sectors when added to the Covid19 mandates to close nonessential businesses, have had devastating economic, and financial effects on America. Sadly, as the mandates are lessening, and businesses are opening again, the Biden administration will claim job creation number increases as a success, but those numbers are not accurate as they are just people returning to previous jobs. Until Biden realizes the best way to bring prices down at the pump is to produce American oil and gas, the unemployment numbers in those fields will remain high.

The fact that America is so heavily dependant on fossil fuels, who would have ever guessed a President would make it their mandate to cancel production of this fuel source. With so many jobs, not just in the oil/gas worker fields, but the manufacturing field as well, all at stake under Biden. We would not have so many devices that we use daily at our disposal if it wasn't for oil/gas refining. Just think where we would be without plastic, we use it in literally thousands of products around the house. Even more dire to our daily lives is our cell phones, and computers. Stop and think how important it becomes to the way we live today. Now let's talk about our dependency for our vehicles, and the heating of our homes. Our dependency is in a wide range of areas, and simply closing off the tap like Biden has done only creates a shortage, not a solution to any of our needs. Fueling up our vehicles has become expensive, very expensive, and why is that you might ask. Well, it has risen drastically due to the fact America must now buy the gas/oil from other countries instead of extract it from the soil within its own borders.

You just can not use Executive Order to cancel something the entire country is so heavily reliant on. This is very irresponsible of the Biden team. Businesses, homes, jobs, and all the way down to the customer and consumer, will have to pay an incredibly higher price, cutting into profit, net worth, money for upgrades, etc. At one point Biden reached out to other countries to produce more oil per day to build a larger supply, hoping to drive the costs down to America. All this did was signal to those other countries that America is in need, and if they want it, they must pay.

I understand that pipelines can be causes of environmental concerns and are not the most pleasant objects to look at. The problem of leaks and oil spilling into the ground is minimal, as safeguards, and standards must be met on a constant basis. I would rather see stricter laws on pipeline manufacturing and usage than cancelling the pipe all together. In many cases, the pipeline is used to bring the oil from the docks where freighters and rail cars supply foreign oil to America and Canada. Many that are opposed to these pipelines aren't aware they exist already in some places, many that are in support don't know they exist either for that matter. The real misinformation is that if these pipelines were of such concern, we would hear about leaks and spills in the news often, as they cover lots of ground.

One problematic pipeline is the Line 5 pipe that runs through the Straits of Mackinac under the Mackinac Bridge. This pipeline since 1968 has spilled 1.1 million gallons in 33 separate spills. In 2018, a 12,000lbs anchor damaged the pipeline, and this is not acceptable. So do activists, and those concerned about the environment have valid concerns? Yes, the answer is yes. That is why we must be very active in finding another source to make our cell phones, computers, and kayaks. Different sources to cut emissions down so we have a cleaner environment. We just can not do it with Executive Power, and with the stroke of a pen to make things better. We owe it to ourselves to make this planet better.

During the campaign of 2020, Joe Biden promised he would be Greener, more about Climate Control, and go after the heavy hitters, as far as pollution emissions. The Green New Deal was the go-to on how we were going to get there, but it came with a huge cost. Most Americans believe we need to be Greener, that there must be some new source we can tap into to fill our needs, but not compromise jobs, products, or the planet. If you research Lithium mines you will be astonished to find they are huge toxic holes in the ground. Those lithium batteries are not the answer to our problems, as they become huge waste problems after the battery dies. The mine itself becomes problematic, how do we fill in or close a mine that enormous? Campaign promises are great, but we need to start looking into a new solution immediately, and before some other country develops new technology that we will in turn have to buy. There is a real race going on to create something incredible, North America must work on this endeavor expeditiously. One thing I will say is, we will not tax ourselves into any kind of answer. Carbon Taxes, increased costs for products, will never amount to any kind of solution, we must put great minds together to brainstorm ideas, not make taxpayers more broke to pretend politicians will discover the answer.

Investments into Green Energy will not be cheap, training alone will be extensive. Before any kind of resources can be put towards training, we must first have something to invest in, and what we will be using to produce Green Energy. We haven't begun to start out on this journey in all fairness, and I would like to see more input from people like Elon Musk, and other leading minds sitting around a new Algonquin Round Table so to speak. Could there be some easy, totally affordable answer just hiding in plain site? I hope so, and we must start by encouraging the conversation about new ideas. Training the workers will be the late stages of this process, hence the reason I am disappointed with Biden, and his canceling of fossil fuel resources so quickly. Are those workers that you say will be retrained for new jobs just going to sit and wait for this process to happen, without any kind of sustainable income to support their families? Did you make the promise to give them first chance at the new jobs, cancel their jobs immediately, then knowingly realize most will seek work elsewhere just to survive. Will they still get first chance at the new jobs if they are now in other fields of work?

One area that will need incredibly large investments once a new energy source is found, will be how existing infrastructure use this new source. Retrofitting is incredibly expensive, and major investments will have to be closely looked into, owners will have to weigh pros and cons of the expenses necessary. Some businesses will surely opt to close their business down if the cost associated with upgrading is too great. This will also affect workers, jobs, unemployment, job creation and staff sizes. Again, the costs usually get placed firmly on the consumer in the end. The new source of Green Energy must take these factors into consideration before implementing anything, unless it is through Executive Order, then no planning is required.

Coal mining has long been a dirty job that requires great commitment. Miners must deal with toxic gases, dangerous conditions, cave-ins, drowning, accidental burns, and explosions. This industry has been on the decline for years, but recently has seen some increases. With the closure of coal mines unemployment again will increase. How will these miners be retrained to have jobs in the new Green Energy industry. Biden is promising workers will be given this opportunity but has no idea of how many employees will be needed. Biden has no ideas at all how it will be accomplished but is hoping Americans will vote for him by making these bold promises. These workers will be waiting far longer than Biden's term in office, and it is a complete disregard of the lives, and families of the workers.

The most glaring hypocritical fact involved in Biden's decision to buy foreign oil over production at home is the willingness for other countries to produce a larger Carbon footprint to fulfill America's needs. Biden has asked those oil producing countries to produce more, putting more oil to market, driving costs down, making less money for those producers, all to combat his failed stance on domestic production. If Green Energy is the deciding factor behind Executive Order to cancel production, and the Democrat Party is fully behind this decision, why would they be alright with increasing other countries emissions? Afterall, are we not all living on the same planet? Do the emissions created in other countries not affect us over here in our part of the world? It is hypocritical to ask other countries to produce oil for America, and virtue signalling to cancel production domestically.

Biden claims job creation in the Green Energy Field will include workers working in the fossil fuel industry currently. How can he make such promises, if he has no real plan, or idea of what form that new field will be in. The callus way in which Biden misleads people to vote for this transition is almost laughable. The transition is not even in the beginning stage, no real plan, or investments have been made to start the process. Sure, there has been a push to buy electric cars, which contain lithium battery components, and other metals that need to be mined like Cobalt. So, if the creation of these batteries is just as hazardous to the environment, is it Green? It would have been a better solution to invest in ideas, and to put together a team to work on Green Energy, but still produce oil/gas domestically. To use Executive Order to make it appear your administration is serious about the transition has been witnessed daily at the gas pumps by those affected most by this poor decision. I could not imagine losing my job with the stroke of a pen, then being told a new field will be offered to me but have zero idea when that day will come. What must those workers be feeling? Investing into the future is a must, but we must not lose sight of current situations. Will we build better ways to collect solar, and wind energy sources? How many sites or future sites will be needed to feed American need? I think Biden should stop promising the world and delivering nothing but desperation.

As I have mentioned already, Biden has been willing to buy oil/gas from other countries, and have their emissions increased to fulfill America's needs. What does this really equate too overall? Well, other than the hypocrisy of cutting jobs to lower emissions but have increased emissions because of others producing for America. There is an unemployment problem domestically due to this poor decision. The other glaring problem is the support and boom to the economy of countries like Venezuela, Russia, Iran, Saudi Arabia, and Qatar. Not only does this hypocritical strategy of Biden's turn a blind eye to emissions it seemingly turns a blind eye to terrorist ideology, and human rights violations. Again, asking the question, would it not be better to bolster American jobs, and economy? The prices skyrocketing in the USA was happening before Russian invaded Ukraine, but the White House, and namely Jen Psaki, blamed those high prices squarely on the invasion. When you rely on other countries to fulfill your needs, be that in any field, you subject yourself to supply and demand. Simple economics at work here, if America wants oil and gas, they simply must pay what OPEC sets as pricing. If the supply is greater than demand it's cheaper, if it's the reverse, it costs more. Both Canada and the United States are sitting on vast amounts of oil and gas reserves but are not utilizing them fully.

In the last decade a huge push has been made to produce energy through solar and wind turbine sources. There are a few problems with this source of energy creation, and I feel they outweigh the positive.

1. Eye sore or unpleasant to see.
2. Endangerment to birds
3. Human illness
4. Recycle after life span is reached.
5. Cost trade offs – more energy to build than generates.
6. Life of equipment

So, I think for me the biggest disadvantage to both solar and wind farms is the way they look. Let's start with solar farms, they are usually built in open fields, and upon completion, fill that field with panels. They take away from the natural look, or the beauty of nature in my opinion. Some homes have installed panels on their roofs, which is more aesthetic, but other homes have large panels in their yards to produce energy for the grid. I fully understand the idea behind harnessing the sun's energy, but not every yard can house large grids to collect it. Personal use, or houses set up to contribute to the grid is a little bit different than filling entire fields with panels. In smaller more rural areas, where green spaces are more abundant, filling the odd field is not as critical. In more urban areas where space is limited, and especially green spaces, it becomes very critical. I would rather see a field turned into conservation areas, or parks rather than solar fields.

Wind farms are more visual than solar farms because they can be seen from long distances. I find wind farms to be less of an eye sore, but they become very obtrusive as their size can block views from existing houses in some locations. If you have built your house for the view that can be seen from inside or from a deck, and windmills get built near you, it can limit those views. In some areas wind farms

are being built in the water, on shorelines, and on low level moun-
tainous areas. These areas can be quite picturesque, but that lessens
with the erection of the windmills. Birds are severally affected by the
windmills, and so are bats. Now I'm not sure how many birds are
killed by the blades, but the air pressure change closer to the turbine
damages their lungs, same with bats. Each wind turbine kills around
five birds and twelve bats per year. Ontario has around 2,577 wind
turbines, so that equates to 12,885 birds and almost 31,000 bats. So,
to understand how many birds and bats are affected in your area find
out how many wind turbines you have, then do the math.

In many cases, humans are finding negative effects from wind turbines on their health. Symptoms include dizziness, headaches, and
sleep disturbance, but there has been no scientific evidence found
to date that supports these claims. That is not to say that people are
making up these symptoms, or that they are not feeling these effects,
and attribute them to the wind turbines. If there is an air pressure
change near the turbines, that can most definitely affect a person not
unlike the birds and bats. Depending on how close you live to wind
turbines, there is some noise associated with the blades turning, and
this could also play a role in how people are affected by turbines.

Today we are trying to be more environmentally friendly, and
our landfill locations are part of that process. Recycling is a major
concern when it comes to windmill blades, as there is no real way
of recycling them. The used blades become objects that get buried
and will not break down and become environmentally friendly
over time. So, if it takes more energy to produce windmills, and the
blades need replaced after a certain time, but those blades become
landfill problems, are wind farms a better solution? The same could
be said about solar components once they are no longer useful. With
the creation of large solar fields, we are looking at the lifespan of
those solar units, and what it means when parts need to be discarded
and replaced. What will we do with the components that are not
environmentally friendly.

The increase in electric car demand is great, and vehicle manufacturers are truly making great strides in being more environmental concerned. Again, what do we do with the used Lithium battery after it is no longer useful? Lithium mining is not a great process, leaving large unusable pits in the earth, and Cobalt mining is also needed to produce these batteries, and other vehicle parts like brakes. We need to invest in how to reuse or recycle the parts not currently able to be recycled, and we must focus on how we can put the earth back after mining has taken place. Before we invest, and build more and more cars, or wind, and solar farms, we need to stop ignoring the inevitable future concern, and face it head on.

To continue production of materials that are already identified as potential concerns, defeats the purpose of green energy itself. By not addressing future concerns and issues and turning a blind eye to a crisis we have not traded for a better solution. We must put as much effort into all the areas of concern, or we will suffer greatly for our ignorance.

Chapter Six -
Poor Infrastructure Policy

Now Biden's Infrastructure plan, or Build Back Better, was poorly designed from the start and even his own Party couldn't get behind it to have it pass into legislature. It mostly consisted of rewarding Blue States that on the build up to the 2020 election, burned cities in protests and riots. Now it shouldn't come as a surprise to anyone that the Biden/Harris administration would reward these cities for allowing this destruction, because during the run up to the 2020 election while these riots and fires were burning, there was few calls from Biden to stop this behaviour, and Harris posted a link to financially support the release of those arrested, posting bail for them. So, instead of focusing on infrastructure that would help the country, like finishing the border wall, or other projects, Biden was focusing on unilateral rewards for those States that did little to quell the chaos on their streets. This was not lost on the majority of Americans who understood the poorly veiled plan.

Let's first talk about the cancellation of the Border Wall Project that Trump started. This wall would have created a real boost in employment and created a major safety net for those border agents dealing with illegal immigrants trying to gain access to the United States. Instead of finishing the wall, Biden decided to stop the build, causing unemployment to rise, and created a major crisis at the border, to which neither Biden nor Harris planned visiting. The biggest problem for me is the hypocrisy of the Democrat Party for making the border a huge media story under the Trump administration, when the number of detained people was a fraction of what the Biden administration is seeing. Biden's administration is actively working on making the border an even larger problem with policies, that embolden thousands of migrants to head towards the US border, with the hope of gaining access. The fact that we have party faithful media coverage, and a lack of real journalism today is allowing the Biden Presidency a pass on accountability for the border crisis, the very same media that spent hours covering Trump's border policies.

There has been lots of talk about how people can cut through the wall or dig under it or even use ladders to climb over with little effort, so why spend money building it? Well, if this was the case would they not be doing that now in those places that the wall already exists? CNN's own Jim Acosta took a crew down to the border when Trump was in power and was hoping to prove a point that the Democrat side was falsely stating about the wall not being effective. Unfortunately, what Acosta proved was that the wall had zero people there trying to get over it, or around it. Essentially proving the wall was indeed effective in securing the border. If the wall does nothing else, it helps those border agents do their jobs with more security, and safety than a border without a wall. The sheer cost of ICE rounding up illegals and sending them back to their home countries validates the cost of the wall, it would essentially pay for itself in a short period of time. This would be a great place to spend infrastructure money, and it would benefit so many people, not just financially, but also for their safety. There is little hope of Biden finishing the wall. One reason, he needs the illegal immigrant vote to counter the Republican support, which is why the Democrat Party is fighting to give voting rights to noncitizens so strongly. Secondly, it would mean admitting the Trump administration was right, and that a border wall is a necessity. Both reasons are poor excuses to avoid what needs to be done. Only now has some talk begun to be heard about finishing parts of the border wall. This will eventually lead to the entire wall being finished I hope, and the securing of the southern border, also ending the Democrats use of illegals as counter votes to the Republican numbers. If you must rely on those votes coming from noncitizens, that means you have lost the support of American's that can legally vote, or at least enough votes to support your agenda.

Another area hurting by Biden's poor infrastructure decisions is the oil industry. Biden has openly stated he will transition away from fossil fuels for green energy, or renewable energy sources. This is great, and if he planned to invest in this transition, it would see growth in the infrastructure. Sadly, Biden has decided to cancel fossil fuel extraction, and rely on other countries for supply, increasing the cost to Americans at the gas pump, home heating, and demand companies increase their development to return costs to normal. Yet another example of poor decision making, but renewable sources must be found, we all agree on that. No decision to cancel something depended upon by so many could ever be mistaken as a sound decision, yet here we are. Trump himself stated before he left office that if Biden follows through with his plan to cancel extraction, it will cost Americans at the pump, even stated $7/gallon. Many Democrats are declaring renewable sources are our best choice to combat inflation and high costs, but what sources, and is there any work being done to build these sources. I guess we are just at the "talking about it" stage, because I see no immediate answers for how Americans are going to re-enter the workforce, or how costs will be coming down anytime soon. And Pete Buttigieg, Secretary of Transportation, telling American's they can stop feeling the pain of gas prices by buying an electric car shows how much the Democrat Party, and the Biden Presidency cares about what American's are dealing with daily.

Now another section that was included in the Build Back Better bill that I disliked was the clause that churches were not allowed access to the funds. Why would a church, which is a building like any other building, not be allowed access to funds that would allow them to get updating? What could build back better than faith? The people doing the work on buildings, carpenters, roofers, windows, flooring, and more, are all the same people that do that work on non-religious buildings, so why discriminate against churches? The Biden administration who claims to be for unity, or so they say, look to be leaving a certain group of voters off the help list, and they are often, Republican voters. Now, maybe it's because churches are tax free status organizations, but churches often depend on parishioner donations for upgrades and repairs. So, would they not benefit greatly from this help, the answer is yes. The people doing the work on churches would benefit from the work as well, so with zero negative scenarios to giving funds to churches, the Biden administration is showcasing a prejudice towards churches in my opinion.

With all the talk of green energy needs, where is there any real investments being made, and where are the green energy sources and training being done? Biden has visited the Saudi Arabian Prince to talk about giving more oil to the Americans to lessen the toll on people buying gas but was told no chance. So, if green energy is so important, why is America begging other countries to supply them, and help them, but America is unwilling to help Americans? Why must the oil rich countries around the world be given even more money, but American workers, and refineries are closed and laid off? Well, the answer is very simple, the Biden/Harris administration is making the worst decisions possible, and there is no sign of them starting to make good ones any time soon. We need to transition into greener energy, but we must find one or two that is better than what we have been relying on like wind and solar. The real race is on for someone to invent or create the best sources of green energy, and that is where I would like to see investments from Governments around the world. I would also like to see countries working together to benefit the entire planet and showcase true unity.

Maybe we should be looking and investing in better ways to refine oil. Look into better processes that take the crude oil and find ways that will leave less carbon footprints until we further develop other green sources of energy. We have such dependencies on oil, gas, and by-products of this industry like plastics, that we will need to find greener ways to make cell phones, and plastics at the same time as energy sources. This will take a lot more than just signing into action an executive order, and saying to a camera, "promise made, promise kept", but then throwing America into a high inflation, low employment, gas price hiked recession.

Schools would be another great investment; many schools are outdated and in poor shape. Technology in some areas is lacking, and students are falling behind in a world so dependant on it. All students should have the best chance at gaining a full life, with education in small towns being the same as those of large cities. What greater investment could there be than in our future leaders, workers, inventors, and doctors? I will touch on education later in this book, but wanted to talk about the building of schools, and the investments to upgrade technology under infrastructure. Investing in schools that build key elements of today's student's abilities to compete technologically is very important. Having the greatest resource, the internet, available and those tools to utilize the internet. We would see a huge return in the very near future for this investment. If Joe Biden can leave over a billion dollars worth of equipment behind in his failed Afghanistan pull out, he can surely invest that into education resources, like schools, and technology.

One place that we should be looking to change for the better is transportation. We should be trying to look into greener ways to improve public transit. Converting buses, and trains to greener or electric should be a great starting place. Some cities have started this process, and more could be done to transition to a better savings to the taxpayer. Creating a better cross country trans-portation system is a bit further away, we should be investing in better ways to utilize solar energy to charge trains. The top of each rail car could be fitted with solar panels that charge the batteries that are powering the train. There are lots of possibilities available if we would invest in finding new ideas.

Across the United States there are millions of roads, and many have bridges or over passes. Many of these overpasses are in need of repair or replacement. Same with bridges, and Joe Biden has promised to replace those bridges. This is a great use of infrastructure money, but within the USA and Canada we have some great steel plants making the best steel in the world. One of those steel mills that produce maybe the best steel in the world is Algoma Steel in northern Ontario's, Sault Ste. Marie. This quality steel should be used to create new bridges, and overpasses and not inferior weaker and cheaper imported steel. Taxpayers' money should not be spent on something that is not up to the most rigorous standards, and the Biden administration should remember it is also an investment into American's safety as well. For it was the unfit state of these bridges and overpasses that caused deaths and made Biden visit locations of tragedy to begin with.

Making sure the water system and supply to every city and town should be a priority. Yet there are cities like Flint, Michigan that needed major upgrades. The one thing that everyone can agree on is we all need good, clean, water to drink. Upgrading water systems for those cities lacking safe water to drink would be a great place to boost infrastructure spending. I would like to see this spending over giving rewards to those cities that allowed fires, looting, and riots to ravage their cities, then while it was going on pretend it was peaceful protesting.

The real hard part of infrastructure spending is where do you begin? You could argue that the problem starts with those in charge locally of each problematic area, like Flint, Michigan. Or you could argue that the problem was funding shortages given out at the State, and Federal levels. Blue States should not be given priority over those States that are Republican run. Cities and those in charge should not be given a reward for the most absurd behaviour that showcased zero concern for people's livelihoods. Infrastructure spending is always a key element to the success of any President and rewarding those States that are already in support of your administration does not guarantee re-election. Any President that has had great success in their infrastructure spending has been able to do so without being partisan. It is very important to represent the entire country and build the country as a whole.

Chapter Seven –
Inflation

What Is Inflation?

Inflation is a rise in prices, which can be translated as the decline of purchasing power over time. The rate at which purchasing power drops can be reflected in the average price increase of a basket of selected goods and services over some period of time. The rise in prices, which is often expressed as a percentage, means that a unit of currency effectively buys less than it did in prior periods. Inflation can be contrasted with deflation, which occurs when prices decline and purchasing power increases.

The Causes of Inflation

An increase in the supply of money is the root of inflation, so when Joe Biden tells reporters that it has nothing to do with his policies, and his spending, he is not telling the truth. The war between Russia and Ukraine had nothing to do with the rise in inflation either, which Joe Biden also claimed was the cause. Knowing that big spending bills from the government is the number one reason for inflation does not take an economics degree, and when more and more bills are being introduced, even though inflation is skyrocketing, there must be an absolute limit. Democrat Manchin killed Joe Biden's Build Back Better bill, and that was a great start. The Democrats are Hell bent on spending abundant amounts of money, and it will cost Americans over the course of years to come. Every day American's can see the root cause of inflation, so it doesn't matter that the White House blames other sources, and Trump, it isn't being fooled.

Oil and Gas extraction has been halted, which puts the dependency of the United States on fossil fuels, squarely on the producers from other countries. Why would the Biden/Harris administration halt production of something the USA is so heavily dependant on? If you find an answer to that question, send it to me so I too can try and understand this inflation causing blunder. Yes, by buying crude oil from other countries they can in turn control the price, which Joe Biden visited Saudi Arabia in quest of obtaining extra oil from their reserves. But not before releasing millions of barrels of oil from the US oil reserves and placing it on the world market in hopes of lowering the price. China was the beneficiary of that oil sale, and it showcases that poor decision making has no limit for this Biden administration.

Now with the price of oil going sky high, the ones that feel the biggest crunch are those consumers buying gas at the pump and heating their homes. Businesses are feeling the cost increases and watching profit margins shrink daily. Not just the price of oil, Biden is spending absurd amounts of money in other areas as well. He has given Ukraine 4 to 5 billion, continually calling for and trying to cancel student debt, and flooded trillions into social programs, and infrastructure. Now the unfortunate aspect of the infrastructure Bill, Biden is hand picking how it gets spent ultimately.

The biggest problem with Joe Biden's spending Bills, and thankfully some did not pass the vote in the Senate, is that they affect the inflation level significantly. When asked about the spending habits of his administration Biden has continually blamed Russia's invasion of the Ukraine for all his problems, but not his spending. Biden even lashed out at reporters asking about his spending causing inflation to worsen, he fired back at them that Government spending has no effect on inflation. The very root cause of inflation is Government spending. So why does Biden get a continual pass from those reporters in the mainstream media who's job it is to report to America what is going on? If you ask me, the Biden/Harris administration needs to be called on numerous things, but it's not happening.

So, what are some key points about Inflation.

1. Inflation is the rate at which prices of goods and services rise.

2. It is classified into three types: demand-pull inflation, cost-push inflation, and built-in inflation.

3. The most used inflation indexes are the Consumer Price Index and the Wholesale Price Index.

4. Property owners may be in favour of some inflation to raise prices of their assets.

So, to understand best how inflation works we can break it down to cost. One unit of money, ($1) buys less units of product when inflation is higher.

The more money Biden floods into the system, the more the rate of inflation will rise. The more the rate of inflation rises, the less your dollar will buy. With this loss of purchasing power, it impacts the cost of living for the public which leads to a stalled or negative economic growth. With Joe Biden my view is that there has been a sustained inflation occurring because his money supply outpaces economic growth.

Let's now talk about a few of the types of demands that cause prices to increase or decrease.

Demand-Pull effect,

Demand-pull inflation occurs when an increase in the supply of money/credit stimulates the overall demand for goods and services to increase the economy's production capacity. This increases demand and leads to higher prices. When people have more disposable income they tend to spend freely, which can lead to increased prices. A good example of this would be in areas where the more affluent live the prices of things are higher for the same goods and products found elsewhere for cheaper. Prices are adjusted by those sellers to reflect the incomes of those shopping there.

Cost-Push Effect

Cost-push inflation is a result of the increase in prices in the production process inputs. This is especially evident when there's a negative economic effect to the supply of key commodities.

Built-in Inflation

Built-in inflation is related to expectations or the idea that current inflation rates will continue in the future. As the price of goods and services rise, people expect a continuous rise in the future at a similar rate. So, workers may demand more wages to maintain their standard of living, some places this is called cost of living allowance, or COLA. These increased wages result in a higher cost of goods and services, and this continues as one factor effects the other and vice-versa. Workers at plants or other facilities maybe demand higher wages when profits are higher, and market values are high. Of course, this is hoping the market for such products are not volatile or cyclically price driven. COLA is always something both current workers, and retired pensioners are concerned about.

The inflation that Joe Biden has faced is directly linked to his policies and spending. That is as true a statement as you will read. No matter how much spin doctoring he and his team try to use to misinform America, it is directly related to his spending. The people suffering the most are people just trying to make a decent living and combat his skyrocketing prices. All the while combating his unemployment in major areas. Workers from the border wall and the oil fields are without jobs and suffering with less wages, and those few wages that they receive buying less and less goods for their families. No matter how much Biden pretends this is not happening, these families are not being fooled into believing the USA has the strongest economy in USA history like the White House had announced. It's absurd that an administration would state such nonsense and then even more absurd that the media has not asked the tough questions about why this would be falsely claimed. The everyday American is feeling the devastation every time they enter a store, and in a lot of circumstances when they get to the store the shelves are empty. I wonder does Biden think Russia caused the shortage of baby formula.

Disposable income is something that the Democrat Party has little concern for. Under Barack Obama, and the passing of the Obamacare or the Affordable Care Act, people were funding their own health care. This expenditure is a great debate piece, as you could argue the value of healthcare vs. what uses disposable income could afford a family. Nevertheless, people were not allowed in most cases to keep their existing health insurance like Obama promised and the middle class are now responsible for the bulk of the funding for Obamacare. Obama moved the lower limits, and the upper levels, to include a wider range of people that would fit into the funding supply. I have zero problem with the upper limit changes, but the lower-level changes had devastating effects on family's disposable income. This meant that any upgrades to the home, new car, University, sports, clothing, family trips, and lots of other things were out of the realm of reality for millions of Americans. Same with Biden's spending causing inflation that has not been seen in over 40 years, Americans are paying more for everything, and cutting back on those same things. The shortages on the shelves showcased a new level of dysfunction by an administration, all the while trying to pass shortages off as the greatest economy ever. Disgraceful and sad, as Americans continue to suffer.

The people most affected by inflation are those people on fixed incomes. Those people who are retired, or on social assistance, and are unable to supplement their income by doing extra work, or side work. Their income is fixed, and when the costs go up, their income stays the same. Having to decide on heating your home or buying groceries is a travesty, and no one should be in that position unless they have created it themselves. With small increases to COLA based on the CPI.

What Is the Consumer Price Index (CPI)?

The Consumer Price Index (CPI) measures the monthly change in prices PAID by U.S. consumers. The Bureau of Labor Statistics (BLS) calculates the CPI as an average of prices for goods and services representative of total U.S. consumer spending. The CPI is one of the most popular measures of inflation.

1. The Consumer Price Index measures the overall change in consumer prices.

2. The CPI is the most widely used measure of inflation.

3. The CPI is based on an index covering 93% of the U.S. population.

The very bottom line is that without the Republicans having majority of either the House or the Senate at the time of me writing this book, the Democrats will continue to push for more and more spending hurting the American people more and more as well. The midterm elections coming up in 2022 will be a huge necessity for the Republicans to gain majority to crush foolish spending on even more foolish policies. The Biden administration sending million upon million to Ukraine for their war with Russia is admirable, but they refuse to address the southern border crisis in their own back yard. Shelves stocked full of baby formula at the overflow facility on southern border, but consumer shelves are empty. Having investigations into Border Agents use of whips that was unfounded from the beginning of the accusation, showcase the lack of decent decision making from this administration. Now, after two years of refusing to admit the need there is finally talk of Biden finishing the border wall, as predicted by many on the Right, because illegals are showing up by the bus loads in DC. I will discuss the border wall further in the next chapter.

Chapter Eight –

Immigration

To have a chapter devoted to Immigration we would be amiss if we didn't start by talking about the much-debated border, and the need for a border wall. Donald Trump ran on the promise that he would build a wall along the southern border, and once elected he made good on that promise. Now many on both sides of the political field have spoken about the necessity of the wall, so I will give my opinion. When Trump was in the White House, the media and Democrats made the border one of the biggest issues on a daily basis. Many Democrats like AOC even took pictures and film crews down to the facility that houses those caught entering the country illegally. The main difference is how those on the Left see the term illegal. Democrats call for the lack of police, call for the closure of jails, want voting rights for illegal citizens, and even support low or no bail. The stance on those being housed in the facility became a media and Democrat talking point about how those people were being treated. Coining the terms, "kids in cages", and "concentration camp", and having those terms be broadcasted and projected to Americans daily. The associating of Trump's immigration policies with evil terms like cages and concentration camps was to align Republicans with inhumane behaviour. Only to ignore the situation completely after Biden took office, and his numbers inside those very same facilities increased by hundreds of percent. So why and how could Democrats be so interested in those people crossing into the country, and how could their view change to the point that it isn't even an interest to the Democrats? Well, the answer is easy, when the Democrats are not in power, and the Trump administration was seeing positive results from the border wall, they tried to turn the tables on that success by using negative wording to always associate that success as negatives. This is a very effective tactic, low and without moral fibre, but effective none the less. So, when AOC was photographed doubled over in pain at the thought of those people being mistreated, she seems to have overcome that grief now that her Party is intensified that suffering by hundreds of percent. The Biden administrations decision to finish part of the border wall is only a start to the wall fully being finished, as it is the best means to controlling the flow of those illegally entering the country. The hypocrisy is not lost on American's and the Democrats have only now noticed the problem because bus loads of those illegals started to be sent to New York, and Washington by Texas Governor Abbott.

The real reason the Biden administration has turned a blind eye to those illegally entering the country isn't even being hidden or cloaked. The Democrats are trying to give voting rights to those people illegally in the United States and are hoping for support as they continue to fear monger them by saying the Republicans will deport them. Another great tactic by the Democrats, but also, a very morally bankrupt tactic. Causing a situation where people feel they will be given this freedom and having them walk to the border in the thousands without concern for safety only to benefit on election day is disturbing to me greatly. The lack of concern once the Democrats took office with those peoples live has been on full display as AOC, Biden, and Harris have not visited the facility since Biden started his term in office. The media has also forgotten about the situation and has dropped any negative association with the now called, "overflow facility". Why the change in imagery by the media, especially since the same problem exists but is now much, much, much worse?

Not only does the Democrat Party welcome those illegal citizens, but Biden's administration wanted at one time to give them $500,000/ per person upon entry. This seemed to be a ridiculous, and openly blatant strategy to gain voter support among those illegals but was a huge issue with everyone else. Once the negative backlash was starting to be felt by the Democrats, the policy was scrapped. The Democrats aren't interested in removing those illegal immigrants from its soil, as they continue to call for the dissolving of ICE, Immigration and Customs Enforcement. Which costs the taxpayers billions annually, so it seems concerning that the Democrats want to dissolve something, then cause the number that ICE deals with to increase exponentially. The very important job ICE is responsible for is the overall safety of the country, and instead of creating policies that work, or supporting construction that helps significantly, the Democrats decided that the best strategy would be to go after the people responsible for that safety. If the Democrats are to give voting rights to the people ICE are removing from the country, then the Democrats will have to stop ICE from performing that duty.

The people crossing into the United States without legal process are not all criminal people, but there does exist among those entering that are very dangerous people. The process of selecting skilled workers, and those people wanting to start a better life should be more than just taking down the wall and having them run into the country in the dark. The safety of Americans should be something both Parties are equally concerned with, and the support of those potential voters should not be the only concern. The amount of tax dollars lost each year due to illegal workers not paying taxes, and the cost associated to ICE tracking and documenting illegal citizens is staggering. The answer is not to defund the very organization that keeps you safe, but to solve the problem before it starts. The gut-wrenching situation and safety concerns for everyone involved should outweigh the Democrats want for votes, but sadly it appears to me that it doesn't.

Another factor to having illegal workers in the country is the loss of jobs for American, and for those people wanting to support their families. If people that are not supposed to be living in the country take jobs away from those that are legal citizens, that is a problem.

One that shouldn't be or can not be ignored by the media, Democrats, and American people. The unemployment levels, the homelessness in major cities, those illegals that have crossed and are now living under bridges in Texas, do not need to be increased. Sanctuary cities and States like San Francisco and California are allowing the costs associated with the situation to increase daily. As those living on the street in San Francisco have to be moved and hazmat clad workers need to wash human fecal matter and other garbage from the street for obvious health reasons. The bottom line is, the Biden approach to immigration is failing, and people's lives are being affected gravely.

Each year there is a need for immigration of workers, and an availability for those needing and wanting better lives. The current process is a process that has taken years to develop, and if administrations like Biden's are going around that process or ignoring it, how could it ever be effective. Without strict guidelines and procedures, the people responsible for immigration would be in a state of constant chaos, and confusion. Does the Democrat Party understand this, or do they have any interest in the process at all? Well, it doesn't seem overly concerned to me as they actively work towards intensifying it.

Immigration - process through which individuals become permanent residents or citizens of another country. Historically, the process of immigration has been of great social, economic, and cultural benefit to states. The immigration experience is long and varied and has in many cases resulted in the development of multicultural societies; many modern states are characterized by a wide variety of cultures and ethnicities that have derived from previous periods of immigration.

https://www.britannica.com/topic/immigration

The definition of immigration has in it the word, "process", which means it shouldn't be done via an open border, with individuals running freely into the country.

What are the Four Categories of Immigration Status in the U.S.?

1. U.S. Citizens

2. Permanent or Conditional Residents

3. Non-Immigrants

4. Undocumented

So, let's look at each of the types, and what describes the individual that is associated with each type.

1. **U.S. Citizens** - These are people who were either born in the U.S. or become "naturalized" after three or five years as permanent residents. These citizens can never be deported, unless the citizenship was obtained through fraud.

2. **Permanent or Conditional Residents**

    a) **Legal Permanent Residents** – are those individuals that have obtained a permanent resident card, someone who has been granted authorization to live and work in the United States on a permanent basis. Sometimes this card is referred to as a "green card".
    You can become a holder of a green card a few different ways, two of which are,

        1. Sponsored by a family member or employer.

        2. Refugee or asylee status

    c) **Conditional residents** – are those individuals that have been married less than two years and must apply to remove the condition within two years or the card is revoked. There is a process to which this must be done, and a small fee associated with it through, Petition to Remove the Conditions on Residence (Form I-751).

3. **Non-Immigrants** – who are in the country legally, but only on a temporary basis.

   Some types of Non-Immigrants are,

   a)   Students

   b)   Tourists, and visitors for work

   c)   Fiancés

   d)   Those having protected status.

4. **Undocumented** - People who are in the country without permission, or illegally. They are not authorized to work, and they have no access to public benefits like health care or a driver's license. Yet, these are the very people that the Democrats are helping the most.

Deportation

Deportation is the formal removal of a foreign national from the U.S. for violating an immigration law. This is also a process that the Democrats are trying to change, by fighting through the courts to stop people from being deported.

Chapter Nine –

Social Policy

To start this chapter off I will discuss the two main groups of Conservative groups. Within the Conservative followers there are two main groups that help identify the main focus.

1. Fiscal Conservatives – those who believe that money and costs are the main focal point.

2. Social Conservatives – those who believe our people are our main focal point.

Now, you could not focus on just one of the two main types, you need to have both to be successful obviously. For the sake of this chapter, I will be focusing on the social conservative aspect.

Social conservatism in the United States is a political ideology focused on the preservation of traditional values and beliefs. It focuses on a concern with moral and social values which proponents of the ideology see as degraded in modern society by liberalism. Many followers of this ideology are Christian fundamentalists, and therefore are not in support of abortion, gambling, recreational drug use, or removing prayer from schools. This group tends to have very widespread levels of that Christian focus, and as such, can become very debated within its own followers.

A lot of Left leaning groups, and followers misrepresent Social Conservatives as ALL being against LGBTQ+ rights and therefore try to label the followers as hateful. One thing that must stop in the United States, and around the world is the labeling of people without any knowledge of what individuals stand for. It only takes a few minutes to conversate with each other to find out what we are like, why not take that time and stop being judgemental towards each other? An old saying stays true on hate, "hate corrodes the container it is carried in, don't be that container". I heard Al Simpson say this at the funeral for George H. W. Bush, and it changed my outlook forever on being angry towards those that cause me pain. We are all given one vote every election cycle, and if we choose to vote based upon our beliefs or our prejudices, there is no changing that. Choose wisely!

Today we are seeing a huge upswing in people "identifying as", or saying they feel more like something they don't visually appear. Now this ideology is very confusing to some, and when talking with people going through the process of finding what they feel most comfortable identifying as, it appears they often become engaged in heated debates. If the person trying to find their identity is confused, how could anyone engaging with them about the subject not feel that same confusion? We are not responsible for the aiding of others to find their identity, unless we choose to help and have been asked first. I will say that some people that identify as things other than human cause me more confusion than those looking for their best fit among the choices humans have. Those people identifying as wolves, or furies, and howl and mimic the behaviour of the animal leaving behind the human behaviour, is difficult for me to fully understand. The one thing we must remember is that we are not being asked about our views, and if they choose to behave that way, it's their life. Identifying has changed so much over the last few years, and I feel that under a Democrat administration there is more focus given to this movement than under Republican administrations. For example, when Trump was in office the main focus was on a false Russian Investigation, tax witch hunts, Stormy Daniels, and failed impeachments. The Left was very focused on finding ways to remove Trump, but on little else. Trump remains the main focus of the Left even after leaving office, which must be taken as a huge compliment by Donald Trump, as he is so important to them. How one identifies when socializing is a personal freedom, and no matter how confusing it may be to others, if it is your friend and they ask you to accommodate them this action, will you? Now just because someone chooses to identify as something, you are not obligated or obliged to play along. It is a two-way street, if you identify as a wolf, not everyone is going to go along with your change. Making everyone, or demanding others accommodate your identity is the same as making everyone around you be your faith when in your company. We haven't the right to oversee others' rights and freedoms, that is a huge over extension of expectation.

Gender identity is the largest change I feel to our social interactions. When we interact publicly with each other there are circumstances that arise where people mis-identify others. If you are born a male, but identify as a female, there will be those circumstances that others will verbally call you male. You can correct them and ask them to identify you as you prefer to be identified, but there is still no obligation by others to do so. It is the same as someone changing their name, if someone changes their name from their first name to their middle name because they feel it more suits them as an adult, their friends will struggle with this change. It doesn't mean they disrespect you; it is just an association of that original name with your face. Likewise, when we see what appears to be male or female, we associate those pronouns without malice. What must go away, and is meant with malice is the term, "it", or "thing", and there is zero room for that ignorance.

Speaking of pronouns, a new thing that I have witnessed is when people introduce themselves, or when they are attaching descriptions on their social media platforms, they use their pronouns. For example,

D.L.Bailey

Author

He/Him pronouns

Vice President Kamala Harris did this even described what she was wearing at the table. This can be seen in two different ways.

1. It gives the people in the room a chance to use the preferred pronouns of the person speaking before hand. This will cause less chances of insulting or offending others. It is a great way of breaking the ice for some.

2. It puts the pressure on the other person to use language or conform to your wants over their freedom of choice/ speech. Again, we are not obligated to do what others demand of us, we are all given freedoms. It boils down to our own willingness, and some will oppose others pronoun choices.

The mainstream media, and followers of the Left like to associate hateful words, and terms with those people on the Right. Don Lemon once called all 74 million voters for Donald Trump as KKK sympathizers. And The View cast had to apologize for saying protesters outside of a Turning Point USA event were part of the event. The associating of negative, or hateful wording to describe people on the other side of your political viewpoint is no different than misusing pronouns. There is no legal obligation for using terms that describe others nicely, but there are laws that prohibit depicting hate groups with non hate groups. The problem with this behaviour goes well beyond depictions, it creates an aggression publicly where people feel the freedom to attack others without any knowledge of the person being attacked. We have created an environment where we don't like when people associate our gender, but we feel free to associate hatefulness without evidence. The level of accountability must rise on behalf of our news, and journalism, before we can fix this associating of others' intentions. Adults don't act that way, and if we want to raise children to be well behaved adults in the future it must stop immediately.

Perhaps the largest divide in our society today is based on race. I have no hate towards others based upon skin colour, but I understand some people do. For the very reason that lives are lost each day based upon hate, I will keep this section small because it would deserve a book all to itself to even start to explain this divide. I would like to say that we can not allow people like Don Lemon to paint all people on one side with the same brush, and label them all hateful. Likewise, we can not allow the news to do the same, storylines should not be permitted to associate one view as positive or negative. Just report the story, don't add, or subtract personal views, or agendas to the report. That is why we lack the faith in our mainstream media reporting the truth. We must all do a better job of calling out hate, all hate, and speak up for those enduring this, embrace each other.

A new form of silencing, or racial profiling that I will mention is something called Progressive Stacking. This is where non-white students are given preference, and non-male. The idea behind this thinking is that those shy or otherwise not openly comfortable talking in class are the ones called upon or given preference over the others. This has so many things wrong with it I'm unsure of where to start. If students have paid their tuitions, and are unable to answer, or ask questions in class based upon their skin colour or gender, why would anyone go to that school? If you are only allowed to, "hold space" for others to have their say, what is really being taught to those individuals? Once graduates of this ideology make it to the real world of business will they succeed as executives if they only hold space for non-white co-workers? The answer is no, they will not succeed, and all students, and all questions should be given the same level of importance. You will never defeat racism by using racism. Also, how will non-white, female, shy to begin with students feel if the white male students are only allowed to talk if it is to compliment them. I can envision a classroom setting where mocking, and anger are used in this complimenting, also sarcasm in the form of, "well if I were allowed to talk". This is not and should never be confused as educating. Which brings up the word, "progressive".

Progressive - has many different meanings, and descriptions, but for the purpose of this book here are two that relate.

1. happening or developing gradually or in stages; proceeding step by step.

2. (Of a group, person, or idea) favoring or implementing social reform or new, liberal ideas.

https://www.google.com/search?client=firefox-b-d&q=progressive+definition

> Woke (/'wouk/ WOHK) is an English adjective meaning "alert to racial prejudice and discrimination" that originated in African American Vernacular English (AAVE). Beginning in the 2010s, it came to encompass a broader awareness of social inequalities such as sexism and has also been used as shorthand for American Left ideas involving identity politics and social justice, such as the notion of white privilege and slavery reparations for African Americans.

> https://en.wikipedia.org/wiki/Woke

So, what is the difference between progressive and woke? There are little differences other than the term woke is more descriptive of what social aspects need changing. Most Republicans or Right-Wing people would admit there is need for changes to how certain groups are treated or have been treated. Most would admit racism is wrong, but this is the group that brought freedom to slaves and gave them voting rights under Abraham Lincoln, and his Emancipation Proclamation. The Democrats try endlessly to depict Republicans as the Party of racism and the KKK, when in reality, they were the Party of the KKK and voted 100% against slaves being free, and voting. So, the Democrats have essentially progressed from a hateful Party, but are now calling the Republican Party a regressive party, that has gone towards the old ways of the Democrats. Which is a very low political tactic on behalf of the Democrats, with the use of the mainstream media, and social media, to appear as the only choice for those of non-white, and other social groups, because they are the only Party that is not racist, or prejudice.

One area well debated and talked about is the trans community, specifically, trans athletes. The social acceptance of those people that identify as trans is far more prevalent than the acceptance of those trans athletes. Biological males, that identify as trans, performing in female sports, has been very common in the last few years. The main objective of those opposed to trans athletes competing against women is the advantage testosterone gives the trans athlete. The muscle and skeletal systems are in most cases, advantageous to biological males. While those that are in favour of trans athletes performing against female athletes don't always admit there is an advantage. I do feel that if a biological male wishes to compete against female athletes, and identifies as a woman, they must take estrogen or a testosterone blocker of some sort to even the playing field. The hypocrisy towards female athletes versus trans athletes is that biological women competing in Olympic sports must take testosterone blockers to lower their levels, but trans athletes are not required to take testosterone blockers. So, to recap, women's levels of testosterone ARE measured, and used to punish female athletes for a fairer playing field, but biological males identifying as female have no such testosterone level limits. I feel that such an advantage will eventually remove all biological females from holding Olympic records or finishing in medal rounds triumphantly. I love watching Serena Williams play tennis, she is an extremely gifted woman, but if she competes against the men, she would not be triumphant.

One other thing I would like to mention about this, "woke" movement is how it is being redefined and encompassing more under its umbrella. One such area is changing the word pedophile to minor attracted person. The name change is an attempt at lessening the negative stigma to a less judgmental one. The reality is, the Left does not see this group as people who hurt children, that are attracted to those individuals that can not consent to such acts as sexual behaviour. I will discuss more about children being over sexualized in the chapter education. I do understand that we are all human, I understand that people have impulses, but children need our protection, and we should focus on their safety, not the words we use to describe the people that hurt them. Instead of changing how we refer to pedophiles, maybe we should offer more counselling to them before children's innocence gets stolen.

Equality - the state of being equal, especially in status, rights, and opportunities.

"An organization aiming to promote racial equality."

Much debate has taken place over equality recently, and one of the main focal points is pay gaps between male and female employees. This is a huge debate subject, and the calculations used to judge the pay gap is skewed at best. Equality or equal opportunity is not being fought for in every field of work, and the factors that make up ones pay, especially at top level jobs is based on individuals. Now I am not saying that pay gaps don't exist, far from it. I am merely stating that the data used to depict this gap as an overall gap across America is skewed.

The last section I want to highlight about social policies is violence, and I understand that I have talked very little about the Democrat platforms related to this subject. I left out Democrat policy and wrote about the social changes because the Democrats endorse most of these changes, and place significance to them. The violence that we are seeing across North America towards Conservative minded people by those of Liberal and other societal groups is uncalled for. Having opposing opinions towards any subject is a great opportunity for growth, and learning. Whenever you have lost an argument, you have learned something. It is not a chance to react with anger, and bitterness, but a time to be mindful that there are always two sides to a story.

Attacking someone for wearing a MAGA hat, or a Republican pin is not justified. In past protests we have witnessed people striking others with bike locks, over an opinion difference, appalling behaviour. We have lost our empathy towards each other. Protests, and riots being endorsed, or downplayed to, "mostly peaceful", is not healthy. If being Progressive or woke embraces this violence, and lack of empathy, then it needs to be extinguished.

Chapter Ten –
Weak Crime Stance

Some Democrats are calling for the closure of prisons and want to see less people being charged for crimes. This includes Joe Biden who doesn't consider drunk driving a felony charge. Democrat Attorney Generals across America are not doing their jobs properly, and this is very evident in the crime rates in those cities. We can look at New York, Philadelphia, LA, and Chicago just to mention a few. Record numbers are leaving New York for Florida and leaving California for Texas. So much so that California has lost electoral numbers and Texas has gained them. So, why if there is so much evidence to prove the weaker the crime stance the greater the crime level, would any sane person fight for even weaker stances? Well, the reason is simply votes. The Democrats are hoping for an increased number of voter support from promises to make life easier for those criminals. California is wanting to close prisons, limit probation to two years, and most Democrat States have lesser bail, because bail is somehow racially profiled now. Bail should be set upon the severity of the crime, not the race of the person committing the crime. In this chapter I will discuss many points about Biden's weak crime stance, and how it is creating major chaos across America.

One aspect is the time given for violent crimes seems to be lessening and repeat offenders that should otherwise already be locked up, are out committing more crime. This is evident by Kamala Harris tweeting support for Minnesota Freedom Fund that collected funds to pay bail for those rioting during George Floyd protests. Maybe she should have taken the opportunity to call for a stop to the riots, and the devastation being caused. Could anyone imaging if a Republican called for, or tweeted a link to support rioters? Imagine V.P Mike Pence setting up a twitter link for anything that caused such destruction and devastation to people's livelihoods.

With a weaker stance on length of time for violent crimes criminals are more emboldened to commit more violent crimes, because the risk is minimal, and probation and bail is set lower. This creates a perfect opportunity for the criminal, and we have seen the results on the news stations over Biden's time in the White House. Things will not get better as the southern border is allowing unvetted criminals into the country, prison closures, Democrats calling for prisons to be abolished all together, and AG's being weak on their stances. California has a three-strike rule for violent criminals, and it isn't being adhered to. So, is the hope of votes worth all this? I think the very clear answer is NO!!!

A very troubling pattern we are seeing is the group smash and grab style robberies of department stores, jewelry stores, grocery, and expensive clothing stores. How are stores to prevent such robberies? What can a store owner do against a mob, and what can a store owner do if the ruling Party sees this group of criminals as a low threat? Petty crime may seem like a low to minor inconvenience to some, but the store owner seeing a decline in their ability to pay bills and feed their families, sees it quite differently. Not to mention the business aspect of insurance. How many insurance claims can one company put in for this style of robbery before it has their insurance cancelled? What happens when a store owner takes things into their own hands to deal with this petty crime? Can store owners defend themselves against intruders and attempt to save their merchandise from being stolen without fear of being prosecuted? Will the Biden/ Democrat AG's see the same low-level threat of these store owners the same as the criminals? Will the store owners face more severe consequences than those criminals committing the robberies? I think once we look at this further, we will have more questions than answers. The truth is crime is skyrocketing, and it is directly related to the Democrats policies on crime. And make no mistake, if a store owner takes matters into their own hands, the Democrats will punish them to the full extent of the law. The would-be criminals will be treated as victims by the Democrats.

Now along with store owners having their stores targeted, and robbed of their contents, there is also a safety aspect to these rob-beries. If you are caught inside one of the stores being targeted by these group smash and grab robberies, you are in a very dangerous place. The store owners are in danger of being hurt, and so are the employees. Often children are inside shopping with their parents, and the factors that make this worse just keep adding up. So, I again ask the question, is it worth it for some votes? Along with the safety of everyone involved, store owners will not be able to withstand such continued robberies, and over a very short period of time will be forced to close their stores. What would prevent the robbers from coming back once the stock has been replenished? It certainly won't be the weak crime stance that the Democrat Party has towards the criminal element.

Public safety is the biggest side effect of this weak stance on crime. Whether it's the store owners, or the shoppers, or the security per-sonal in some stores, people are affected gravely. It doesn't stop at just stores, it has been witnessed at parades, trains, front porches, intersections, gas stations, and it's getting worse. Public safety is not having those people intent on causing others harm walk freely among them waiting for opportunities to arise. I will discuss further in the chapter about defund police stances, but for now I will mention it as it also is a Democrat stance to lessen the police presence at the same time calling for less prisons. In Los Angeles the train system carrying freight, and parcels is being targeted by looters, and the tracks are covered with opened boxes from stolen goods. The safety of those people working on the trains is not being looked at by allowing these criminals free reign. Now no one is calling for lengthy prison terms for small crimes, and no one is saying that Republican States have zero crime. Of course, crime is something that is always going to be a problem, and never going to be abolished completely. How a governing Party views crime/criminals is the best starting place for a positive change to how things are presently being done.

Another side effect of crime is cost to consumer. If stores have to pay more for security, and for costs to how they store and sell goods, the consumer will eventually have that increased cost put towards them in sales cost.

So, let's discuss what increases costs to the consumer.

1. Insurance
2. Security
3. Relocation to higher rental buildings
4. Additional secure display cabinets
5. Costs associated with security upgrades to windows/doors.
6. Restocking stolen goods
7. Repairs for damages to stores.

Focusing now on the affects that the criminal element cause towards the unsafe, and dangerous environment. If criminals are caught committing crimes and given the proper time and punishments for those crimes, there should be a program set up to start rehabilitation. Only through proper rehabilitation will those committing crimes be given a real chance at changing their lives around. So where are the chances for those criminals to have a better life? Where does the Democrat stance on crime take into account the quality of life those committing crimes are living through? If prison is not the place for criminals, and the streets are seeing skyrocketing violent crime numbers, when is there an admittance of failure? Calling for less prisons, less time for crimes, less police presence, less bail, and less probation time continues to astound me, as it is a complete failure to consider people's lives, and safety. The record number of repeat offenders highlights this failure perfectly. If given the chance for rehabilitation, and that rehabilitation comes with some deterrent to commit future crimes through the loss of their freedoms, with incarceration, people will stand the best chance at a better life.

Areas that should see more investigations.

1. Politicians making money off stocks.

2. Politicians making money off foreign countries.

3. Family members profiting off foreign jobs.

4. Politicians using positions to influence criminal investigations of their children.

5. Politicians selling uranium rights for donations to personal foundations.

6. Politicians using personal foundations to fund campaigns.

7. Politicians allowing foreign spies to infiltrate government offices.

8. Politicians' treatment of others sexually

9. Politicians' history of offences

10. The IRS focusing on Conservative groups.

11. The FBI (Due to the mishandling of Hunter Biden laptop, Russian Collusion, etc.)

12. The origins of investigations based on false claims.

Areas that need more funding not less funding.

1. Police

2. Prisons

3. Rehabilitation facilities

4. Mental health care

5. Training/ education for those incarcerated.

I feel that the situation that highlights the need for a change best is California. In California the effects of weak crime stances are marked by a mass exodus for other states. With this mass exodus comes more electoral college votes for Texas, as they received so many of these spurned Californians. So, what has been going on in California to bring about this exodus? Here are a number of factors.

1. Prison closures
2. Weak view towards crime
3. Looting of freight trains
4. Street violence
5. Sanctuary State
6. Sanctuary cities
7. Attorney Generals not using three strike law.
8. Homelessness
9. Unemployment
10. Personal freedoms

Prison Closures will actually.

1. Place more criminals on the streets.
2. Increase the crime levels.
3. Affect the safety of the public.
4. Place more work on the police.
5. Affect businesses.
6. Affect homeowners.
7. Increase insurance costs.
8. Drive people out of California

9. Not allow help for rehabilitation

10. Destroy California

Sanctuary States and Cities create in my opinion.

1. Housing for the criminal element without deportation

2. Allow violent criminals to continue behaviours.

3. Create laws to protect State and Cities from prosecution.

4. Make taxpayers financially responsible for illegals.

5. Destroy public safety.

Again, the weak stance the Democrats are taking on Immigration, or the Southern Border is affecting the crime levels we are seeing across America. With Blue States like California near the top of the list. If the Biden administration does not begin to reign in the southern border crossings and take a much better and more realistic stance on how those criminals are punished, American taxpayers will be the ones that are most affected. Never have I heard of any administration openly allowing people to gain access without regard to who they are, and in mass numbers, to the country. The fact that immigration and public safety and the crime level, goes hand in hand, the Biden administration is failing miserably. Having the White House Secretary tell people the border is secure, or that crime levels are good does not change the facts of the situation, neither are acceptable.

For the Democrats to be calling for prison closures, and open border views they are not representing their constituents properly. Elected members of both the House and Senate are to represent those people that voted them into office. Upon getting those elected positions members of the House and Senate are not supposed to openly work towards administration failures without regard to the safety of voters. American's work hard for their money, and to be preyed upon by criminals that continuously are given no reprimand for their actions is infuriating. To see violence, robberies, theft, murders, carjackings, home invasions, and assaults increase at the same time Democrats call for even less punishments showcases how out of touch Democrats are.

Now I realise that not all Democrats are in support of closing prisons. The ones pushing this agenda the most are Rashida Tlaib and Ayanna Pressley. Their hoping to pass a sweeping bill that will see the mentally unfit, that are currently incarcerated be given the proper care, by closing the prison all together. This will put rapists, murders, child molesters, and other violent criminals back on the street. So why not focus on identifying the mental health inmates and giving them the proper care? Well, it goes back to the vote. Tlaib is taking the most heat for this idea, but Attorney Generals, and prosecutors are showcasing this same agenda. Governor Newsom in California, and Democrats that created sanctuary States and cities supporting this agenda. Beto O'Rourke wanting an open border supports this agenda. And any Democrat that does not verbally speak out against this agenda supports it quietly. There is zero reasoning behind prison closures, let all criminals free to prevent mental health needs is not at all reasonable. If no reasonable excuse can be offered, the only thing I can see for this is votes. A very desperate and unsafe excuse for more votes. Who and how will the Democrats place the blame for the crime increases? Maybe this will all be Vladimir Putin's fault? Or Donald Trump's, or both.

Illinois State Sen. Kimberly Lightford, D-Maywood (ILGA.gov) was the victim of a carjacking in Chicago along with her husband. Lightford is the Illinois' Democratic state Senate majority leader, and Lightford was instrumental in passing a bill ending cash bail earlier this year, putting criminals on the streets. Even after seeing firsthand how poorly conceived, and how much of a failed approach this is, she still supports it. HOW?????

Maybe you the reader think I am for mass incarceration, or maybe it could be perceived that I am against giving people second chances. Well, I am for the safety of the public first. Understanding that any time you commit a crime there should be consequences for that action, and upon the criminal not the public. Understanding repeat offenders, and those that are unable to be rehabilitated need to be places away from the public for everyone's safety, the criminal included. There is no simple answer, there is no easy way of saying people are not all interested in treating others with decency and respect. Incarceration is not always the right path to rehabilitation, but walking the streets is definitely not the right way either. I am for prison reform, not closure, lengthy time for violent crimes, and for the rule of law.

Chapter Eleven -
Defund the Police

Perhaps the most visual attempt at vote grabbing is the Democrats stance on Defund the Police. The Democrats are putting the safety of the public behind their own interests, and behind the want for power. It is not very difficult to understand that those people that choose to commit crimes, and especially violent crimes, need to be removed from society for the safety of the people. An attempt to explain how those criminals need to be out on the street by Democrats has not gone over well in most of the USA. By reducing the police presence on the streets, and by allowing criminals the upper hand by cutting funding how could this equate to safety? Do the Democrats calling for this truly believe themselves that this is a reasonable thing to instate? The absolute truth is this, if there are less police to arrest criminals, and the Democrats start to close prisons as some have stated needs to be done, the crime rate will skyrocket even more than it has already. To create such a chaotic environment that would see criminals freely reeking havoc on the everyday American, and all for their votes is purely evil in its design. To care so little about hard-working people, wanting to live their lives without fear is horrible.

Now do the Democrats that want less police set the example for this in any way? NO, absolutely not, they actually employ their own additional security because they themselves know the crime rate is up significantly in their ridings/districts. So why advocate for something that is already not working? Well, a few things are being attempted or being sought after.

1. Votes from criminals otherwise incarcerated.

2. Votes from those supporting less police.

3. Votes from the groups advocating for this.

What is happening in reality, by the Democrats pushing for Defund the Police.

1. Loosing support from police unions

2. Loosing support from police officers

3. Loosing support from law abiding citizens

4. Creating unsafe communities

5. Showcasing Democrats unconcerned view of Americans

6. Showcasing Democrats lack concern for criminal rehabilitation.

7. A continued lack of concern for American businesses being affected.

8. Bolstering support for opposing stance on crime and police needs

Now not all Democrats are advocating for a defunding of the police. They are not the problem, but what is problematic is the few Democrats and mainstream media that are trying to say that the Republican Party is the party advocating for Defund the Police. We have witnessed a real shift in accountability lately, and the Democrats and the MSM are not hiding their agendas from Americans, but rather ignoring facts and reporting false information. There is no one on the Republican side calling for a defunding of the police, border agents, or any other agency that protects America.

So, in order to call for the defunding of police, there must be some reason for the call. That reason is the vilifying of the police officers as racists and attempting to paint all police officers as the same. Are there police officers that act in careless, and hurtful ways? Yes, there are some police officers that should not be allowed to perform the job. Now, let's talk about the majority of men and women that put that uniform on and make our cities as safe as they possibly can each day. Those men and women that leave their homes, and families unsure if they will return home after their shift. That deal with some of the most violent, and Hell bent on destroying our safety for personal gain. That protect us, so we can live our best lives. I could not write about the Defund Police movement and not write how much I respect and admire those men and women who put themselves in harms way for our betterment. We can not and should not assume that an entire group of people, are all hateful because they wear the same uniform. We do not assume all doctors are negligent because one doctor maybe makes a mistake during an operation, we should reserve judgment for those officers that continue to perform their jobs greatly.

What Defund the Police is creating is increased violence towards police as the Left vilifies them. Police officers already deal with an incredible amount of violence daily, how on earth could anyone support increasing this. By increasing the violence towards police, maybe the Left is hoping to get their wish as police officers retire earlier than they had planned or quit in some cases. The demand for police has never been higher than in recent years due to the increase in crime under Democrat rule. In many cases, the cities that advocated for and implemented reduced police budgets like New York are already reversing that stance as crime is at incredibly high levels. I think everyone can agree that it is quite clear, increased crime is directly caused by less police presence on the streets.

Some on both sides of the political field are seeing a usefulness in having an increased presence of social workers, and psychologists to work along side the police. I agree with this, but not at the expense of having the police on the scene. By placing a social worker to deal with a violent criminal suffering a mental breakdown, both people become increasingly unsafe. We must not become ignorant of reality to seem more compassionate. The ultimate safety of the public, and those police/social worker/ psychologists must be first and foremost. Every step possible must be taken to ensure the people suffering breakdowns are given the utmost respect and help possible at the same time.

As I have already written, there are some cities that jumped on the defund idea only to have to reverse their stance in short time due to crime levels. There does not exist a city that has defunded their police services and had crime levels drop showcasing a need for this insanity. Some cities that have defunded their police services are.

1. Minneapolis

2. New York City

3. Cook County Chicago Ill

4. Portland

5. Austin

6. Baltimore

7. LA

8. Milwaukee

9. Philadelphia

These cities are not experiencing success in their defund ideology, and the citizens of these cities are the ones being affected the most. This voter grab in reality is costing everyday Americans their lives, and if there isn't a reversal of this poorly designed failure more lives will be lost.

Let's focus now on tourism levels as a result of defunding police services. Those cities that have an ever-increasing level of crime are going to see a very visual decrease in tourism numbers. People are just not going to go see those places and cities that may end in their own demise, or safety being compromised. This goes along with my earlier statement that businesses are not a factor Democrats supporting Defund the Police are concerned with. Democrats did little to stop the riots and looting of businesses before the 2020 election, the media falsely claimed it was "mostly peaceful" and the businesses are still suffering because of it. So true is the fact that high crime affects businesses as well as personal property so why are the businesses and people not a concern equally for both sides?

Biden has repeatedly talked about crime levels, and in his State of the Union Address he mentioned funding police not defunding so why are Democrats still calling for it in major cities like New York. It is a matter of saying one thing and doing another. Calling for funding police in addresses to the entire country is to gain support from those against defunding police, while calling for defunding when talking to those regions in support of it. I believe this is called being "two faced". The truth of the matter is that no politician should endanger police officers' lives with rhetoric like defunding the police. This behaviour places the onus of blame on the officers' and not the criminals. Do we really want to live in a society that has very little security and law enforcement? Well only if you plan on a life of crime would this sound like a good idea. Are the Democrats really that desperate for votes that they would pander to those criminals, and pander to the people wanting less safety for everyday citizens? The answer sadly, is yes, they are pandering for those votes. So, if the desired goal is less police and the crime levels increasing by the hundreds of percent, why is there not more outcrying from the people in those affected regions and cities? Same reason we never heard from those residents living in the areas rioted and looted, they were never asked, or interviewed. The media is telling us it's a great idea, and the Democrats are calling for more defunding, but the people living in these high crime areas are not given airtime to voice how they feel. The real sad truth is the Democrats know it is unhealthy, and the wrong approach to crime, but are still going ahead with their plan anyway. It showcases a lack of judgement and concern for voters' safety, while pandering for power, at all costs.

If the Democrats truly felt that less police presence was the right path, or was the answer to any problem, they would not spend hundreds of thousands of dollars on private security for themselves. Why the private security if it's safest for everyone else to have no police around? In some cases, the violent crime is up 13% and climbing, while unarmed lesser crime is on the decline. This would indicate that more criminals that otherwise would not have used a weapon to commit crime, are now emboldened to do so. With little police in some cities, and with the call for less bail, less prison time, and less parole, what is preventing those criminally inclined to refrain from becoming more, and more violent? What will prevent those citizens trying to live their lives as normal from becoming victims of violent acts?

The answer will be that those citizens will rise up against the criminal factor and use vigilante like tactics to create what they might believe to be safer communities. In reality, all that has happened is crime, and violence has increased even more. So, what is the answer? The answer is to stop sending politicians to Washington that create this chaos with their pandering for votes. Stop voting into power those politicians calling for the demise of our safety and using tax money to pay for their own safety that no one else in the country can utilize. Every day citizens can not afford their own private security, and how would that look if we all went about with a team of security guards? The truth is the power is in the voters' hands.

The best way to combat this defunding of the police departments is very clear.

1. Vote out politicians calling for less police.

2. Vote out politicians and DA's that call for no bail.

3. Vote out politicians that want less parole lengths.

4. Vote out politicians that enable the criminal over taxpayers.

5. Vote out politicians that want to close prisons.

6. Vote for politicians that put you first.

That brings me to the next point I want to bring up, voting.

Chapter Twelve –

Voting Rights

To believe that voters should not have to show some form of identification before being allowed to cast their vote is to not truly believe in democracy. So many other countries around the world have in place a national identification law requiring them to prove who they are before being allowed to vote. So why would it be considered racist, inflammatory, or somehow wrong to ask that same basic law be followed in the United States? Well, it has been a law since the 1950's, and most of the States follow a form of id law. The fight to remove the requirement seems to be the same as regression instead of progression. How could we not require something so simple, as showing identification, before utilizing a huge personal freedom like voting.

States that require some form of identification before voting

Photo ID required (strict): Georgia, Indiana, Kansas, Mississippi, Tennessee, Arkansas, and Wisconsin.

Photo ID requested (non-strict): Alabama, Florida, Montana, South Carolina, Hawaii, Idaho, Louisiana, Michigan, Rhode Island, South Dakota, and Texas.

Non-photo ID required (strict): Arizona, North Dakota, Wyoming, and Ohio.

Non-photo ID requested (non-strict): Alaska, Colorado, Connecticut, Delaware, Iowa, Kentucky, Missouri, New Hampshire, Oklahoma, Utah, Washington, Virginia, and West Virginia.

No ID required to vote at ballot box: California, Illinois, Maine, Maryland, Massachusetts, Minnesota, Nebraska, Nevada, New Jersey, New Mexico, New York, North Carolina, Oregon, Pennsylvania, Vermont, and Washington, D.C.

With twelve of the sixteen States that don't require id to vote being Democrat, and a call from the Democrats to ease restrictions on who can vote, we will see a battle brewing before next election. A few Republican Governors have brought about new voting laws that have made it more difficult to vote with out id, we hope to see more restrictions put in place. Georgia was one of the newest states to change their laws, and there were false claims made even by Joe Biden himself to the media. So, what did Joe and Democrats say about this new bill?

1. Republicans won't allow food and drinks to be handed out, (I agree it shouldn't be as it could be seen as buying votes.)

2. Republicans won't allow water; (Self-serve water is available actually.

3. It was not mentioned by any Democrat that early voting was expanded.

4. Out-of-precinct voters can't vote, (They have to vote after 5pm.)

5. It eliminated the signature-matching process for voter ID requirements, (True and rightfully so.)

6. Drop boxes would be inside voting stations and (Again rightly so.)

7. Portable and third-party polling facilities are banned, (And yet again, rightly so.)

If you look at the changes to the laws in Georgia, the changes are reasonable, and make complete sense. Restrict the availability of outside sources influencing votes, expand timeframe to vote, vote at your local polling station, fast track voter checks by using id, drop boxes inside secure areas to prevent any question of ballot stuffing, and eliminate portable hard to regulate polling stations. All these things are completely fine to people interested in participating in a properly run election. If you fight against these simple changes what could be the reason? The Democrats pushed a narrative that the Republicans were trying to suppress votes, and that it was somehow racially targeted. The truth is the voting system is needing a heavy overhaul, and each State should use the same format. In Canada the election cycle is much shorter and is uniform across the country. The population difference is greater in the United States, but I feel the biggest problem lies in the fact each State gets to set their voting rights. If there were a uniform process that every State had to follow it would be much smoother run.

The Democrats want to allow non-citizens the right to vote, and decide who the President, House and Senate representatives are. This is ridiculous, imagine going to any other country and trying to vote in their election. The simple, and correct answer to this voter grab technique is, "NO"! With the Democrats not wanting to address the out-of-control southern border crisis, and in turn giving those illegal immigrants the right to vote, it is maybe the clearest example that the Democrats are trying to stack the deck for votes. A few examples of the Democrats not examining the outcome of their decisions but going ahead with vote grabbing techniques are.

1. Open southern border, not addressing chaos,

2. Giving illegal immigrants voting rights

3. Weak crime stance

4. Defund police.

5. Student load forgiveness between $300B -$500B

6. Taxpayers on hook for student loans

7. Build Back Better rewards, Inflation Reduction Bill rewards.

8. Media not calling false claims about voter law changes.

9. Dissolvement of the Electoral College

10. One person one vote system, population density would cause huge tensions.

These are just a few things the Democrats are using to swing voters in the next election. Hopefully, voters see through the smoke and mirrors, and understand that none of these attempts will increase opportunities for everyday American's. If the Democrats want to stand in defiance of people showing ID to vote or stand against secure locations for drop boxes, what is the real reason. So, let's take a look at some of the things that people are required to show ID for.

ID required for,

1. Alcohol purchases

2. Cigarette and tobacco purchases

3. Driving

4. Political Party events

5. Club memberships

6. Airline tickets

7. Traveling across borders

8. Banking

9. Purchasing a vehicle

10. Purchasing a home

These are just a few things I can list. So, if Democrats are against voters showing ID why are they not against purchasing alcohol or tobacco with ID use? The answer is simple, those things listed above don't affect elections.

Biden ignited controversy during a radio interview with Charlamagne Tha God on "The Breakfast Club." Where he said during the campaign for President 2020, that Blacks considering voting for Trump are not black if they do. He later apologized for such rhetoric, but it showcases that the Left is willing to use any means necessary to swing votes. Playing one race against another in this fashion is incredibly low. With such actual disregard for Black voters' feelings, or concerns, Biden was hoping to cement support based solely on skin colour.

"If you have a problem figuring out whether you're for me or Trump, then you ain't black," Biden said.

There is no room for this kind of cavalier attitude towards racial issues, and especially from the side saying we need to find, "UNITY". How will unity be found if you use race to grab votes?

In order to be elected President a successful challenger must achieve 270 electoral votes. In the last few years under Biden, California has lost votes and Texas has gained votes. President Ronald Reagan only missed out on 13 electoral votes when he ran against Walter Mondale in 1984, the electoral map from that election was almost entirely red with Republican wins. We need Reagan back.

The Democrat Party has also tried in many ways to remove the Electoral College from being used for a single vote count, most votes win policy. This can not happen and must never be allowed or most of mid America would not even have a say in elections. Resulting in those States being given zero importance from Presidential hopefuls. States like California, New York, Florida, and Texas would make the decisions for the entire country. The Democrats wanting this change to voting is hoping to gain power as California, and New York are almost always Blue. Campaigning would only be done in high population cities/ States and promises to only those cities and States would incite anger from the rest of the country. A new civil war would break out, and rightly so.

The Electoral College was used all the way back to 1787, and the one person one vote was thought to be not a good way to elect the President, as 60% of the population in southern States were black slaves unable to vote. So, if this was the case back in 1787, does it not still stand today? If there exists a chance that areas that are not equally populated, will have less say, and not be truly represented, it must be made fair. If Roger Sherman and Oliver Ellsworth knew this back in 1787 then surely, we can understand fair representation is necessary. Even in Canada where the population is significantly less than the USA, the use of popular vote to select our Prime Minister is not used.

There are 105 seats in the Senate, whose members are appointed by the Governor General on the recommendation of the Prime Minister. The House of Commons has 338 seats, held by members elected by citizens who vote in general elections or by-elections. The Government originates in the elected House of Commons. According to the principle of constitutional monarchy, therefore, the Queen rules but does not govern.

https://www.elections.ca/content.aspx?section=res&dir=ces&document=part1&lang=e

In order to be elected Prime Minister of Canada with a majority Government, a candidate must win 170 seats of 338 seats. A minority Government can be formed with less than 170, or a coalition Government with multiple Parties forming Government with a combined majority of seats. The popular vote is not used, each electoral seat has different populations. If an electoral seat in Ontario has 600,000 eligible voters, and one in PEI has 20,000 eligible voters, each seat has the same outcome. This is very similar to the Electoral College and is the fairest way of electing either a Prime Minister or a President.

In Canada and the United States there seems to be a push from the education system for a very Liberal governance, and children are being exposed to the viewpoints of teachers, which must stop. In some instances, teachers have been reprimanded for speaking out against Conservatives, and even Donald Trump himself. One case a teacher during a zoom meeting with her class stated her only hope is all Trump voters died before they could cast their ballots. We can not allow our own personal viewpoint to be the only allowed view or we have lost our democracy all together. I will discuss the education system in my next chapter, but wanted to highlight the bias that exists, and how it is another attempt from the Left to influence voter outcomes.

Chapter Thirteen –

Education

Education is being used recently to indoctrinate children with agendas from the Left, and the main areas I will highlight are as follows.

1. Gender
2. Zero tolerance for opposing ideas.
3. Free speech, words vs actions
4. Progressive stacking ideologies
5. Racial
6. Entitlement
7. Parental input removed.
8. Books pushed on children.
9. Over sexualization of children
10. Teachers' ideology pushed, ie All Trump voters must die
11. Teachers' lifestyle pushed, ie Drag Queen show
12. Replacing old school for wokeness

We have touched on gender identity already, so I won't start from the beginning. I don't care if someone wants to identify as a different gender than what they were born as, and it has zero effect on my personal life. I do want people to feel happy and safe, and live the fullest life they can possibly live. Expecting others to take changes in your life serious, or with the same emphasis as you do is unrealistic. So, when it comes to education, and schools' roles in teaching gender to our children will be different for each teacher. Those teachers that are dealing with gender identity themselves will obviously have a different outlook than those that are not. With that being said, it is not up to individual teachers to decipher what they think the curriculum means, but rather School Boards to establish the stance, and that board be accountable to the parents who have children in attendance at those schools.

In some cases, teachers have taken matters into their own hands and set up lessons for as young as kindergarten-aged children about gender. Having an older student start the lesson as a boy, then halfway through the lesson leave and return as a girl. This lesson was not in the curriculum and was not put to parents for approval before moving ahead. The children were mortified and went home incredibly upset only to have the furious parents approach the school to find out how this could happen. The teacher was very clear about their want to teach the lesson and knew beforehand that the parents would not approve, so proceeded without permission. This is not a teacher's role.

School curriculums are very much important to parents, and teachers must also have a say in how children receive education in their classrooms. All my life I have had great teachers', and they have always understood my parents were very much involved with me at home as well as what I did at school. Parent/teacher night was always attended by both of my parents and came with questions and concerns. I feel those questions were taken seriously by my teachers, and my parents always had respect for my teachers having to put up with me in their classrooms. So, how did we get to a place where teachers try to inject subject matter that they know to be combative, and cause parents great concern? We got there by a shift in beliefs, and the importance of our beliefs over others. The best memories I have are of those years from kindergarten to grade 12, where I spent time with the absolute best people around me, and teachers who cared immensely about us.

Today's children, whether any parent or teacher wants to address the issue, are becoming more aware that gender, and gender assignment is something people of all ages are dealing with. I believe teaching children to be respectful of others trying to find that identity is more important than teaching all children they can be whatever they wish. If children are taught to handle the subject of other peoples concerns with respect it will be far greater to their futures than trying to push agendas of either side of the spectrum. In reality, respect is the one subject needing the most room in any current curriculum.

In some cases, children are not being given the same respect if their ideas, social stance, or political stance differs from that of the teacher/professor. There was a case not long ago where a student made a report on his respect for the police, and what they must deal with daily. The student highlighted his respect for police, and it was met with a very verbal disagreement from his teacher. The teacher is allowed her opinion, and she is allowed to voice that opinion, but must not do so in a very disrespectful fashion and berate the student for his opinion. Having a difference of opinion is what creates a learning environment, and that can not be more encouraged than at school.

Other incidents involving teachers being less tolerant of student's political support have also been available because of technology we have today, and some forgetting there are cameras literally capturing our interactions better. If you are in class, online, or attending a group function you can be assured if something happens, it will be recorded. Teachers that wish to remove children from class or not allow them the same audience to be heard should not be in the education field. As a parent, if my child was confronted by a teacher that differed to the point it became verbal in class, I would feel some form of worry about fair marking. If a teacher verbally berates you in class, or online, a natural concern would be, "is my work being graded with that same degree of disapproval". Having a difference of opinion from that of your teacher could be a great learning tool for the entire class. The class could be made into groups based on their beliefs, or support and have an in-depth discussion or lesson, it could be a very fun experience. Having your belief, or stance on a subject be met with a confrontation, or a teacher taking a stance of authority could become very hostile, especially for shy children.

We are blessed in North America with Canada and the United States both having something called free speech, or freedom of expression. We are allowed our beliefs, and values, and allowed to express those beliefs and values freely. Others are allowed to agree or disagree with your beliefs/values but are not allowed to silence or disallow you that right and freedom because it differs from theirs. Teachers are included in that and are not allowed to remove anyone's freedom to verbally express themselves. In the case of the teacher shutting down a student's belief that police officers deserve our respect and admiration, the teacher was wrong to voice her distain for the student's choice of hero. It is her job to evaluate the way it is presented, and to question the student on his choice, but not to express her angst for the police, and berate the student with her opinion of them.

There is a fine line between what is allowed and what crosses the line when it comes to free speech. Hate speech is also a grey area, as some people believe that they have the right to say hateful things under the free speech umbrella. If anyone is trying to pass hate speech off as a fundamental right they have, remove yourself from that environment it is toxic and can not be made better. Hate is hate, no matter how much anyone tries to pass off that vernacular as ordinary language they are wrong. All to often the Left tries to pass facts, and opinion off as hate speech, when in fact it is just a difference of opinion. Some time should be spent in class teaching children what the real meaning of hate speech is, and respect again for others verbal opinions. There is definitely a tremendous amount on teachers' responsibilities in the classroom, no one is saying otherwise, but in those instances where personal beliefs override better judgement, there must be consequences. I reflect again on my own experiences with my teachers over the years, and the incredible discussions had in class on a range of subjects, I remember them positively. Which is what the main goal of education is, make a lasting memory where you learned something lasting. I was also blessed with a class of 32 other children that I feel is one of the greatest blessings in my life. The quality of those discussions was definitely enhanced not just by the intelligence of those other children, but by the amazing people they were, and remain today. The teachers my children have had and continue to have also set the bar high. Acknowledging that not all police officers are bad, also fits here where not all teachers are bad. I am only calling on parents to be involved as much as they can be with their children's curriculum, to alleviate the presence of toxic classrooms.

We must remember always that our words can hurt and can make lasting impressions on others. We can control so very little in life, but we can truly control what we choose to say. If what we have to say is intentionally hateful towards someone else, it really says more about ourselves. Teachers must control what is allowed to be viewed as free speech and hate speech. The classroom should always be a place where children are allowed to express all kinds of things, freely, and without condemnation. Will other children laugh at something you say? Absolutely yes, but hopefully in a lighthearted way, and with no disrespect. Having your best friend turn around in class after you answer and give you that look like you just started speaking another language should be the start of non-stop laughter, not stress.

A professor at a University in America tried to implement something called Progressive Stacking. What this ideology represents is a chance for non-white, non-male, and shy student's the opportunity to speak, all the while white males were to, "hold space", for them. Now, I can see giving shy students some push to try and become more comfortable answering and speaking in class, but the whole thing was wrong when race, and gender became a factor. The

University quickly removed this from being used as it was obviously based on the teachers' personal beliefs not curriculum.

Creating an environment where children of any one single colour, gender, race, faith, or other identifier has preference over the other children will only result in tensions not learning. Universities must make money, and students pay good money to attend classes, with hopes of graduating from acclaimed schools giving them hiring preference. The fastest way to destroy your attendance levels is to create an environment where only non-white, non-male students get to be verbal. The Democrat Governor of Oregon Kate Brown is doing a great job of destroying the education value of her State by making reading, writing, and math subjects no longer a requirement to graduate from high school. Universities from out of State will not be interested or allow students from Oregon to qualify for entrance into their schools without a test or maybe not at all. By lowering the bar for more graduation numbers and calling that a win for her team is not the right answer. Governor Brown should change her mind fast, so students aren't affected drastically by her poor decision. Even businesses will be reluctant from hiring graduates from Oregon because of a lowered level of required education. What business will want a student that isn't able to write, read, or add?

The entire progressive stacking and Gov Brown lower education requirement is based on race. The very side that is saying they will unify the country is wasting time creating race divisions, and in the worst possible place, the classroom. I would not want to have anyone be not allowed to answer a question, only be allowed to stand up and say I did a good job. I would be even more reluctant to answer because of the extra spotlight caused by this. Shy children don't like more spotlight, they actually run from it. Imagine not only are you one of only a few students able to answer questions, you must now sit and answer every question with all the other students staring at you because of this. This student will be short lived in this classroom before dropping it for a different teacher that doesn't use progressive stacking. Also, why would any student that is not allowed to answer

114

attend, participate, or be involved positively? They wouldn't, and parents paying for this type of education should be refunded.

Being told that students of colour are not graduating at the same rate as white students also has nothing to do with their abilities. Making policies or creating lesser levels of education for students based on their skin colour will ultimately have negative affects on everyone. Using race as a way to try and get re-elected or saying that students of colour need extra help in basic subjects is very offensive, and wrong.

Entitlement is something that is getting worse, and with Joe Biden trying to cancel $300 to $500 billion in student debt, leaving taxpayers to shoulder the burden will intensify it tenfold. Many students believe that starting out in the work force with student debt is something the government should eliminate. These same students believe that after first getting hired at a new job they are somehow entitled to the same perks as senior members of the team. The term, "wealth hording", is often used to describe those individuals that worked hard at building a company, worked hard to climb the corporate ladder and built a great life for themselves and their families. This entitled belief that new hires are somehow owed part of someone else's hard work is the definition of entitlement. Why would anyone try so hard to better themselves if in the end, the new guy deserves the financial benefit? Well, that is called communism, and it fails everywhere it is tried. The canceling of student debt for current student's will incite anger among those parents that worked hard to pay for their children's education, or among those student's that worked jobs while attending classes to offset the cost.

In Virginia Governor Glenn Youngkin won based almost solely on his stance that parents have a significant say in what students are taught. His opponent in the race for the Governors mansion was Terry McAuliffe who did not believe parents should have any real say in what children were taught in classrooms. With so many on the Left trying to label parents as domestic terrorists for wanting to have a say in what their children get as far as education subjects, I can see why this became the game changer for Youngkin's victory. Parents have been showing up to school board meetings and reading books that are being placed in school libraries that are very pornographic in nature, along with graphic images of children and adults interacting inappropriately. One mother was told to stop reading the material as the board member said it was offensive. If it's offensive for them to hear it is definitely offensive for students.

Parents should be encouraged to take part in the education of their children. Teachers should be excited about parent's that are engaged with them with the shared desire for students to achieve their best results. Why are there people against this involvement? Why would parents be labelled as domestic terrorists for caring about their children? I think the reason behind this lashing out from the Left towards caring parents is over the material being introduced to students, and how it is being presented as something of merit but is Leftist agenda. Now, before you think you have slipped into a conspiracy theory novel hear me out. Highschool children are being given a pass on subjects like math, reading and writing which trickles down to K – Grade 3 children being introduced to gender studies, trans, and drag queen reading hours, where are the students learning how to read, write, or do math. Children in their first year of school do not need to learn about sex, or gender identity, or what drag queens are. Not saying that drag queens are to be banned from classrooms, but wouldn't you start with Grade 8 student's that have a far greater comprehension of life than kindergarten children? The Left is trying to change the way children at the earliest age are taught, and what they are taught, and unwilling to allow parents a say. Only by keeping parents away from schools, labelling them as terrorists for caring, and using subjects that are no where near what most on the Right agree with, could this ever be accomplished. This is definitely a clear signal that the Left is trying to indoctrinate children to their ideologies, and it must be met with equal resolve.

Parents have their hands full in some areas with teachers that insist on their ideology over curriculum. We have seen the examples on YouTube, teachers calling out student's for believing in the police, teachers telling classrooms that all Trump voters hopefully die before voting. Can you imagine being so careless, and cavalier towards others life, and having zero empathy for life itself, that you wish 74 million people die because they vote Republican. The teachers that try to implement subject matter knowingly behind parents backs to get their ideology into young heads is appalling. In some cases, teachers have talked openly about their own sexual preferences, and gender issues with young children which is incredibly inappropriate. In many of the cases I mentioned there was correction taken by schools, and parents, and I applaud those that did so.

The books available to students need to be better selected, and parents' concerns need to be better heard. Any book that depicts a young child engaged in sexual acts and illustrated by drawings has no place anywhere near a school. How that got published, and distributed is probably the best example of free speech rights, as offensive as I find that, it is someone else's right to tell that story. Schools should know better than to bring it in. We all know that if there was a crazy book in the library when we went to school everyone would want to check out what all the commotion was about. And that is why schools must ensure what children see is appropriate. The difference is how do school board members differ from your value system beliefs.

Once upon a time, the values taught at schools were aligned with those of Christianity, and Judeo-Christian values. Today we have moved away from faith in our schools, moved away from sticking to the same old lessons and subjects and embattled our schools with political agendas. One could argue that for so long the schools were entrenched with the values that were more Right leaning. Times have changed for sure and depending on what side of the aisle you support, you might find it a good thing, or you are in disbelief. After school groups like the After School Satan Club trying to be allowed to operate have taken to the courts to challenge the school board for denying them to be establishment. If allowed by the courts this Satanic club would offer students a range of activities. Those activities would not align well with a majority of American's I believe.

At the University level and College level a very disturbing trend has risen over the last ten years where Conservative groups are not allowed the use of common spaces for meetings. All other groups are given fair timeslots, but when Conservative groups have the meeting rooms booked the other groups block entrance to the rooms so meeting can't be held. Trump promised he would defund those schools that didn't put a stop to such behaviour, and that is the right approach. These Conservative groups were meeting off campus and having their meeting places blocked by the same student's. Teachers and students alike attack guest speakers like Ben Shapiro when brought in to give speeches at school auditoriums. One teacher attacked Michael Knowles telling him that she considered his speech to be violence. A very clear difference exists between violence, which is an act, and saying something you disagree with, which is an opinion. He said it best when he tells her she has no right to be an educator if she doesn't know the difference between violence and speech. So, have we swung so far Left in our beliefs? Have we swung so far Left in our values? And have we swung so far Left in other areas?

We have swung Left, hard Left in our shows we watch, movies we see, and News broadcast to us that is for sure. Being told right is wrong and wrong is right in so many cases. It has become all encompassing, and the media is a huge part of that.

Chapter Fourteen –

Media Bias

As we have witnessed over the last six years or more there does exist a major bias in our Mainstream Media. The coverage and continued assertion of guilt towards Donald Trump over the Russian Collusion and Mueller Report made that abundantly clear. Democrats were given time on almost every channel, and there were endless amounts of guest speakers all focused on how the walls were closing in, or the final nail in the coffin, but in the end, nothing. So, why put in this amount of time only to look foolish after the truth comes out? Political strategy to help the Democrats, by keeping a constant negative view of Donald Trump, that lasted almost his entire Presidency. The media went from promising to produce tax evasion proof, to interference into elections, to impeachment over a call, then impeachment over January 6th. The media never came on and redeemed themselves by talking about how the President didn't let the country down by doing the right thing, just kept going with one negative after another hoping to find something that would stick. Why did they not give as much airtime to the Clinton email scandal? Why did they not talk more about the details of the Sussmann trial? And why didn't all those people angry at Trump for calling Ukraine about Hunter Biden not become enraged when the video of Joe Biden telling people how he as Vice went to Ukraine and told them he wouldn't give them the $1B worth of aid until they fired the lawyer looking into his sons' dealings? That video is a huge piece of evidence that showcases what Biden does to foreign governments.

The other thing people should be furious about is Hunter Biden getting a free pass on everything. Imagine Donald Trump Jr. being a drug addict, not paying child support, making money off foreign boards, flying in Air Force 2 to do business, or having the mayor of a major city, have his wife send Don Jr. $30M. No, instead they tried to make a big deal out of his hunting, imagine......hunting.

With so much to report as far as what the Democrats were doing, I always wonder why the media would work so hard to make up stuff about the Republicans, when the truth is there to be found. Let's just state a few things easy to find.

1. Eric Swalwell dating Chinese spy Christine Fang and having her in his office.

2. Bill Clinton sexual allegations, and subsequent payments

3. Hillary Clinton email scandal, smashed devices, lost emails.

4. Hunter Biden laptop, Ukraine dealings

5. Paul Pelosi stock purchases

6. Hillary Clinton connection to the Russian Collusion beginnings

7. Joe Biden statement showing abuse of power in video about Ukraine and Hunter

8. Maxine Waters telling protesters to stay on street inciting more chaos.

9. Nancy Pelosi not sending in backup on January 6th.

10. Hillary Clinton, Donna Brazile, debate question debacle

I could go on but that is some major stuff to cover. Now it didn't go unreported, it just got a small mention, and forgotten about. Spies, conspiring to remove a President, insider trading, abuse of power, inciting riots, cheating are all some very powerful claims, so why not research them and report the findings. There was some coverage of the email, and Benghazi ordeal when Hillary had to answer for her role in the attacks that killed four American's. Biden should be held more accountable for his role in the Afghanistan pullout that resulted in an additional 13 service members losing their lives. These brave men and women didn't die in vain, and I do not write about them as pawns to showcase my distain for the Democrats. These brave men and women died doing a great service to their country, and what they believed in fully. I have huge respect for service members and am thankful for their service to guarantee our freedoms are intact.

To mention one side that reports all things great on the Left, we must also mention there does exist a news channel that reports all things Right. I admit I follow that news channel on the Right, and I research what they report, and I have not found it to be misleading or wrong. I can not say the same for most on the Left as riots will never be, "mostly peaceful". I think that those pictures and footage of Left leaning reporters standing in front of huge fires, with looting and rioting going on in the background, telling viewers that the protests are mostly peaceful will describe best how our reporting was during that time. We also witnessed reporters standing in a ditch filled with water wearing chest waiters telling America of flooding, while his cameraman stood in shallow water. And reporters pretending to fight gale force winds while two people casually stroll by in shorts and hoodies, hands in their pockets. It's a great selling point, I get it, but come on.

When did we move away from reporters finding news scoops, and reporting to the world the facts of the case? When did we decide we need to have reporters and media outlets that always slant the story to be in favour of one side or the other? We got there because of money, and political views of the owners of the media outlets. People with agendas of their own, wanting to have their party win and look good. We got there because people don't stop watching fast enough to make these owners realize they are fed up. If viewership stopped significantly after being fed a bullcrap story about how something like a riot/looting was actually peaceful, or almost peaceful, that type of reporting would end. Once the money stopped coming in reporting would go back to realistic coverage. I for one can't wait. The news should be reported to us, not have the reporters interpret what we need to hear. It signals to me that real journalism is dead, and that media outlets hire the people willing to say whatever the channel wants.

A good example of media bias could be found when then Prime Minister of Canada Steven Harper visited Israel and Palestine. When he was in Palestine, he was asked by reporters about the evils Israel were committing against the Palestinian people. Then, when he was in Israel, he was asked about the evils Israel was committing against Palestine again. He pointed out that there were two sides to the conflict, and that by asking him both times about Israel's part the media had in fact found a new way to be anti Semitic. The media is no stranger to only reporting one side, but it was amazing to see a world leader stand up against it.

I would like to see as I have already stated, more non-biased coverage from our media. I also would like to see less government funds going towards one source. In Canada the CBC News receives about $1.4B annually from the Canadian government. This seems to be a tremendous amount of taxation to me for a news outlet. What is the difference of someone like George Soros funding a news outlet, or the Government funding. Well, either way it allows for the potential to slant the news towards the ruling Party's favour, or the funding person's political view. With the use of tax dollars being used, other news outlets are not allowed the same opportunities. When Justin Trudeau ran against Steven Harper his campaign promise was to increase money to the CBC, which already gets the lions share, but was a great campaign strategy. If you are promising more money to the main source of information to the voters what chance is there that you will be showcased negatively? I'm definitely not saying the CBC news covered them differently but campaigning to give more money to the CBC was strategic I believe.

I think the clearest indication that the news is Left leaning was when Donna Brazile gave the questions to the Presidential debate to Hillary Clinton. So, what is wrong with this?

1. It's cheating on behalf of the Clinton team.

2. Donna made a poor decision, later apologized for her role, and I believe her.

3. Showcases bias on behalf of a news channel.

4. More should have been done as far as fines, or penalties,

5. Compromises integrity of the debate system

6. Showcases a need for a debate team comprised to formulate and run debates.

7. Gave an advantage to one side to formulate better answers and seem more prepared to voters.

8. Forever damaged reputation of both women in my opinion

One area that the Mainstream outlets seem to show their bias, is in the guest segments. Not just news outlets, but also Left leaning shows like The View also are heavily loaded in the Liberal minded but have only one Conservative guest. Outnumbered, and spoken over during their time to speak, Conservative guests or hosts for that matter are attacked relentlessly. I wonder why any Conservative would go on The View and subject themselves to this kind of treatment. People like Ann Coulter and Bill O'Reilly always seem to do well in these situations, and it makes for some good entertainment. Bill made two hosts leave their own show, just got up and left mid show. Other Conservative guests like Ben Shapiro, Michael Knowles, and Matt Walsh always do a tremendous job of articulating their views, with patience and calm demeanor. One mainstream outlet was known for losing video connection with Conservative guests if they were making good points, using facts that could not be argued well.

The mainstream media did a terrible job of reporting during the Trump Presidency. A few of the things I believe stood out were.

1. Trump's tax forms that somehow got dropped off to the media.

2. Russian collusion

3. Trump's call to Ukrainian President

4. MAGA hat wearing Nick Sandmann's behaviour on the Capital.

5. Fake hate crime's

6. Eric Swalwell role in Chinese spy Christine Fang

I do realize that to have a great news channel, there must be money both earned and spent to create that channel's greatness. I think that the only way to prevent major leaning to one side or the other is to somehow create a board that oversees how things are reported. Now I am not talking about what Biden tried for a week starting up a government board to control disinformation. An actual board of reputable people given the power to hand out fines for blatantly false claims, or for not being forced to clarify stories once they have been proved wrong after the fact.

Ultimately, the real power is in the viewers hands. If someone likes to watch CNN or Fox for their news sources, then they will. I have my preference so why wouldn't someone else. I can not watch some other sources once I research a story I have read and found they have reported falsely. That is my opinion though, and others may not wish to do that. I have had many arguments with people about what they have watched, came over to my house or work and regurgitated the story line as given to them, only to be hit with actual facts about the same story. I truly feel respect has gone from our daily lives in many different areas. We seem to have lost respect for each others' views, opinions, beliefs, and values. Instead, we have decided our views, opinions, beliefs, and values are the only ones acceptable. Same goes for our media outlets at times. We live in a time where there are more ways than ever to collect information, and about more subjects than ever. We can click on the internet and find what is going on in any country around the world almost, and at any time. I would have loved this ability when I was younger and researching a subject would have been incredibly more fun than reading encyclopedias at the library. Don't get me wrong, one of my favourite places on earth is a good library, but as a child the internet would have offered so much more. The problem today is when talking with others that differ in opinion, people use dismissive approaches to information they didn't have. A story backed with facts can not be dismissed by someone who chooses to disagree by saying they don't believe your facts, they are facts. Same goes for stories heard on news channels, if you don't like the reporting one can not say it isn't real because it was on this channel or that channel. Sadly, in many cases the latter has been true though. It always pays to inform yourself about something first, don't trust any one media source for the entire story. Check both sides and give yourself the option of hearing all aspects.

Misinformation and media bias are one and the same, I have decided to create two different chapters to highlight aspects I feel need addressing. There might be some light overlapping of topics and points, but I promise to keep it to a minimum. In this chapter I wanted to highlight the fact that the news channel itself can create news with a slant, or political lean. Where in the next chapter I want to talk about the power of misinformation and what it can do. I do realize that almost all things political have some slant to them. This book is not written without some light slant towards one side itself. The information I have put in both this book, and my first book, Decency and Deception, Encouragement for a Struggling Nation, are my opinion and how I view the actions, and behaviours of the Democrat side during a certain timeframe. The source and the information used for both books have been researched to authenticate my views.

Chapter Fifteen –
Misinformation

The largest problem with mainstream media giving us their version of the truth is that people are not allowed to form their own opinion from having just the facts given to them. People are given the opinion of the news channel and not enough of the facts to have a debate on the subject. An example of that would be when many channels were portraying Trump as a racist, but not giving real examples of when he said racist things. Some media told us that he meant all Mexican migrants, while in reality, he never said all, just that some coming across illegally were bad people. The media was pushing a negative view of the President by misinforming us of what he really said. The narrative was effective as I have had many conversations with people stating that Donald Trump was racist. A simple question on my behalf ends most of those conversations. I simply ask what he has said that makes you the maddest. It's usually right there that most people can't mention anything that they have heard of, or they mention the comment about illegal migrants having some bad people sneak through. If you can't mention anything, how can you be angry? How can you declare a person hateful if you can't illustrate any acts of hatred? This is what misinformation can do, and if you believe the news channel you always watch to be truthful, then you will repeat this information. That is what the media wants from people, get angry, tell this misinformation to people, confront others and label them with negative labels to silence them. But don't engage in fact-based conversations with people that are informed about their beliefs, because you haven't been given any facts.

I mentioned in the last chapter that I believe there should be some form of punishment for misinformation, and certainly for purposefully misguiding people. Biden has been given Pinocchio awards after many of his speeches because of the false claims. Depending on how many times he states a wrong, misleading, or false statement, he is then given that number of Pinocchio's. This is not enough, the President of any country should want to be accurate and truthful, not misleading, and false. I understand that this is a part of politics that exists for all Parties, and all President's, but it needs to be better dealt with. If a news channel is given fines on a constant basis, then further steps will have to be taken to ensure truthful information is what gets broadcasted.

During the Second World War, Germany controlled the information that its citizens were given. The best way to control people is to control what they know. This is still what goes on in some parts of the world. The German people had little way of knowing what was happening to the Jewish people during the war, as they were told what Hitler wanted them to know using Reich Ministry of Public Enlightenment and Propaganda. This ministry was the jurisdiction of the Nazi Party, and headed by Joseph Goebbels, and Werner Naumann. The mainstream media tries desperately to connect the Nazi Party to Donald Trump. Using terms like concentration camps to describe his overflow facility at the southern border but have not used the term since Biden has taken over the White House. Why the sudden change in description? Why would the media not use this term to describe Biden's overflow facility since it has exponentially more people than Trump ever had? Well, the truth is a negative, and evil, association was placed on Trump's Presidency whenever possible. It was true also with other aspects not just the border. The media tried to describe Trump himself as Hitler's equal from many personal aspects. The not so funny thing about the Democrats and the Mainstream Media is that they are using the media to misinform people much like Germany did, while trying to connect the dots between Hitler and Trump. Since that aspect didn't really take a hold on people, it has been dropped and we have not heard it lately. Hopefully, we never see that comparison again. By trying to align your opposition with one of the most hated, and evil people to ever live, for political gains, you lessen those evils and atrocities, and destroy someone unethically in the process. It is shameful, disgusting, and evil.

What are some of the side effects of misinformation?

1. Arguments and family riffs
2. People silence others with accusations.
3. Votes cast with wrong information behind them.
4. Politicians getting free pass on accountability.
5. Reputations ruined.
6. Guilty before trial

Many family arguments have broken out over misinformation and has caused riffs between members which sadly is directly related to the media telling us to be intolerant of others. I will not blame Right or Left supporters for family riffs but only state that I have witnessed it plenty of times, and over politics, nothing personal, and that is the power of misinformation. People choose to silence or remove friends, family, co-workers, and neighbours from their lives because we have become less tolerant of people's differences. Have differences always been present? Yes, they have and that's what makes people fun.

So, let's look at some lives now that have been affected by misinformation.

1. Judge Kavanaugh
2. Donald Trump

3. Nick Sandmann

4. Amy Coney Barrett

Let's look at Judge Kavanaugh, and his questioning before being nominated to the Supreme Court of the United States. Brett Kavanaugh was nominated to fill a vacancy on the SCOTUS and after that nomination from President Trump, allegations of sexual assault came forward. The media, and the misinformation that I align with the Kavanaugh case comes in the form of guilty before questioning. I do not question if Ms. Ford believes Kavanaugh did this act, and I do not question Kavanaugh's claim of innocence. The years between when the act was supposed to have happened and Kavanaugh's nomination was over thirty years. I do question why the media reported from an angle that Kavanaugh was guilty, the slogan, "believe every woman", and the professional made signage that protesters outside the building Kavanaugh was giving testimony in, who paid for that? What else is odd is how a letter sent to Senator Dianne Feinstein and asked to remain confidential ended up leaked to the press. I also question why actress Alyssa Milano sat through many days of trial and spoke repeatedly about how she believed Ford but was unconcerned about a Democrat Keith Ellison who was being accused by his ex-girlfriend and her son at the same time. If it was about women's rights, or about believing every woman, why then was Ellison's accuser not given any of Milano's time. Was she not believable? In the case of Ford vs Kavanaugh there was only her word against his. There were no witnesses that remembered ever attending a party at that location, or on that night. In the Ellison accusation the ex-girlfriend went to the hospital, and had a 911 call as proof, but still no support from Milano. To me it seemed more to do with protecting Roe vs Wade and keeping a potential judge that might vote to overturn that decision, off the SCOTUS, as the main reason for support from those on the Left. I'm not questioning if the women are lying about anything, just how differently the media covered the two stories. I bet most people don't know a thing about Keith Ellison's accuser, and everyone knows Kavanaugh. The two stories were not given the same weighted coverage, and one had a significantly more powerful effect.

So much has already been written about Donald Trump and his alleged coercion with Russians to steal the 2016 election. Years of media coverage telling viewers that proof has been found, and that nails have been put in the coffin, walls closing in, guilty verdicts are imminent. Robert Mueller investigation will uncover Trump's attempt and have him impeached. Democrats like Rashida Tlaib videotaped telling crowds she is going to Washington to impeach the "bleep". The Left had Trump guilty before any proof could be presented because it was a power grab. Never have I witnessed anyone being found more guilty before proof is found by the media and the Democrats alike. It's utterly shameful, and it's plain wrong. Innocent until proven guilty is what everyone in America should be, Donald Trump was not given this by anyone on the Left. Well, the Mueller Report after two and a half years of media blitzing America with Trump guilt, found nothing to proceed on, not guilty. How could the media have gotten it so wrong, and for so long? What happened to the evidence the people like Adam Schiff told America they saw? I mean a President was accused of working with a foreign power to overthrow a federal election. Trump also faced taxation questions and ended up paying more than his fair share. The media used these accusations to project negative coverage, while leaving no room to cover Trump's administrative accomplishments to American voters. So busy telling them that Trump was bad, they forgot to report he had the lowest unemployment in American history among African Americans, and that his economy was thriving. Of course, the media had time to report that Obama is taking credit for Trump's accomplishments, but no one is believing that as Joe Biden is Obama 2.0 and America under Biden is even worse than under Obama. Joe Biden and the Democrats push before midterm elections 2022, where they have decided that MAGA supporters are trying to destroy democracy and are extremists. Even stating that MAGA supporters are a threat to fair elections. This is similar to when Hillary called half of

Trump's supporters, deplorables, racist, xenophobes, homophobes, and other derogatory names.

"You know, to just be grossly generalistic, you could put half of Trump's supporters into what I call the basket of deplorables. Right?" Clinton said. "The racist, sexist, homophobic, xenophobic, Islamophobic—you name it. And unfortunately, there are people like that. And he has lifted them up."

https://time.com/4486502/hillary-clinton-basket-of-deplorables-transcript/

So, why lash out at those supporters with untrue, and misleading labels that are undeserving? The plan is to stop those supporters from talking openly about why they support Trump/Republicans, to stop them with fear of labels. The plan also includes trying to stop fence sitting Americans from voting Republican by branding them as negative, anti-democracy hateful people. It's shameful, and desperation is plainly clear on their faces. Will it work? The media will help as much as possible, but outside of the poorly veiled attempt to demonize the Right, I believe it will swing some people to believing this mistruth. This newest round of attacks comes after Trump's Mar-A-Lago was raided by FBI agents looking for documents. If you ask me, timing a raid on a former President's home, just before midterm elections, where Biden is behind in polls, then attacking MAGA supporters, is familiar. The Democrats had a two-and-a-half-year long investigation into Trump during his Presidency, now as he might be poised to run again, he is under Democrat led investigations yet again. If he is guilty then he should be made to step down, but if he is just investigated for the next few months to sway midterms, then we will know something devious is happening. The question is, if he is not guilty of anything again, how many times are the Democrats willing to look foolish? Did Trump have documents at Mar-A-Lago? Yes, he did, but they knew what he had because they were just there and told him to put an extra lock on the files. Let's just hope we eventually know the truth. Since Trump, both Biden and Pence have been found with documents. Now Trump is seeing indictment charges, with the DA of New York, who seems to be overlooking the crime wave hitting the metropolis, for a political driven attack. If the charges don't stick, or there is a lack of evidence behind these new charges, will it help Trump is 2024?

I don't want to spend too much time talking about Nick Sandmann, and how he was treated by the media and the Left after footage of him was broadcast falsely as the protagonist during an actual peaceful protest on the Capital Hill grounds. He was made to look like a disrespectful and terrible person and the man responsible for causing the tension filled incident was given an interview, as well as airtime to say what he felt. The young man was behaving in a way that any American parent would be proud of. He was protesting his convictions, but doing it with respect, and maturity. What we witnessed from the media outlets, and some Hollywood celebrities was anything but mature, or respectful. Nick Sandmann had footage of the incident changed and altered so that a negative could be broadcast to viewers because he was wearing a MAGA hat. The saddest part of this ordeal is that even people as young as high school age are not safe from the politicizing of the Left and the media. An out of court settlement was reached and Nick has been compensated for being targeted. Aside from financial compensation I hope the offending side offered a heartfelt apology for the event and learned some positive lesson about honesty. The full video of the event did however showcase that there were people acting very inappropriately that day. To highlight my point about misinformation, those people, and the scoop of the story that day was covered up to run a false story about a young man wearing a hat. I can only hope that this incident has not caused the young man to feel he is unable to protest his convictions, and others are not discouraged by the events either. The Left, and the media want to discourage support for those things on the Right, and we have witnessed the lengths they will go to.

Another judge nominated to the Supreme Court that faced sever protest from the Democrats, and the media was Amy Coney Barrett.

She was asked by Kamal Harris questions that would show prejudice and could not be answered. She was asked by Mazie Hirono if she ever sexually assaulted anyone. What a strange question, why would that question be asked, why a person with such an amazing reputation as a mother, wife, judge, and Christian be so disrespected? Well, Hirono did ask that same question of Ketanji Brown Jackson at her questioning before being strongly selected by the Democrats on the committee. The difference was very clear as with Barrett, Hirono asked her if she assaulted anyone, then asked her if she paid anyone in a settlement, then asked her about using the term sexual preference. The term sexual preference she claims is offensive to some people, and questions if members of the LGBTQ+ community could feel their constitutional rights would be upheld by her verdicts. Whereas with Jackson, she simply asks her to outline what she has done to prohibit sexual harassment in her courtrooms. One side is projected to viewers as offensive, and bias, while the other is given an open microphone to showcase her view. To American's watching, Hirono's view of Barrett, and her potential overturning of Roe vs Wade is central to her questioning. I feel that while some have attacked Hirono for her line of questioning about harassment, it is a subject worth asking about, and she should try to ask the question in a fashion that is the same for everyone equally. I feel bad for the treatment Amy Coney Barrett received during her nomination, and was equally impressed by her knowledge, and strength for sitting through it all with composure, and professionalism. Clearly showcasing the reason, she was nominated in the first place. The treatment from outside the questioning was horrifying to witness. Jackson conducted herself well for me until she could not and would not describe what a woman was. Then lashed out saying she was not a biologist.

How do biologists define a woman?

Female (symbol: ♀) is the sex of an organism that produces the large non-motile ova (egg cells), the type of gamete (sex cell) that fuses with the male gamete during sexual reproduction.

So, Jackson agrees with biology, and biologists? Then does she also agree that the true definition of woman is based on biological findings and not gender identity? We don't know, she wouldn't answer the question. Does it matter? Will it affect her verdicts? If Barrett was questioned about her use of a term describing sexual preference, and how some feel it is offensive and could be used against some people. Is it not the same when talking about gender preference, and how some might feel it could be used against them? Is Jackson not lawfully required to use the term for a woman as the law describes "woman"?

Along side those people affected by misinformation there are also others that get thrown into the mix as well. And those people who potentially get negatively viewed by the public, or one side of the equation. People don't always ask for the attention they receive and become angry after because of the fact. Misinformation has so many ugly sides to it, and that is why it needs to go away. It can destroy people, their families, and their reputation both as a husband/wife, parent, or professional image. And in most cases never change that image back to what it should be.

One area that needs to be cleared up I feel is the Jeffrey Epstein and Ghislaine Maxwell trials. Not so much the trial itself, but the client list they kept should be made public. Why has it not been made public, and why has no charges been filed against anyone on the list? There is obviously some reason for the utter silence when it comes to that list, and who is on it. We are forced to focus on what the media insists we should be focused on but somehow, not focused on a list of people doing something worthy of two people being put in jail. They weren't put in jail for nothing, and yet a list of people that used their services is not even mentioned. We need to have that list made public, and we need those people to be made accountable like Maxwell is being made.

Now I have already mentioned the media trying to pass off the rioting that happened before the 2020 election, as "mostly peaceful".

Well riots are not peaceful, they are not lawful, and they should not be supported by either political party. The mainstream media was reporting from on the scene, fires burning behind them, stores being looted, and businesses ruined, lives ruined, but told they are peaceful. Some high-profile politicians even helped bail out rioters by sharing links to places that collected funds for bail. These situations are anything but peaceful and should not be passed off as nothing. Why have we not seen footage of those burned-out businesses after the fact? Why have we not heard from those store owners? If these riots were truly peaceful why not showcase the after math and showcase how those areas look today. These things will not happen, and the Build Back Better bill that didn't pass into power was designed to quietly send funds to fix up those areas without anyone ever seeing how unpeaceful it really was. I wonder why no one has done a documentary on that, or maybe I just haven't seen it. We were told over and over again that nothing was to worry about, nothing to see here, only to witness for ourselves the devastation on the news behind the reporters. Biden should have done more to tell people to stop rioting, and once asked about it he merely said he's not in power. If there is anything that should have brought both sides of the political game together it is combat chaotic behaviour in the streets. If a divide between parties is causing riots, and looting, then both sides need to put the betterment of the country first and stop it. If a war breaks out will one side work against the other in an attempt to look better? Well, that is what happened during those riots, and the media backed them so far as to make themselves look foolish by saying things that are visually not true. To reward these Blue States that rioted, and looted themselves, with Build Back Better funds the Democrats look foolish as well.

The one area that went way too far was the Border Agents, and the accusation of using whips on the illegal immigrants crossing the border. The Border Agents started to use horses to deal with the shear number of people flooding across the border. Even though Biden's White House will tell you it's not like they just walk across. Well, they do, or the Border Agents wouldn't have been accused of anything. The Agents started to see some success with the use of horses, and the media, and the Democrats started to accuse them of whipping migrants. Biden lashed out at these Agents and threatened recourse for their actions. Talking about how awful, and terrible the Agents behaviours are towards these poor people. Well, no proof was found of Agents whipping migrants, and yet there was still talk of discipline coming for the Agents. If the Democrats wanted to focus on something happening at the border, they should look at the number of people coming across, and why it has become a crisis, hundreds of times worse than when Trump was in power.

Chapter Sixteen –
Religious Freedoms

One of the greatest freedoms people enjoy today is the freedom to choose their religion. Free to follow, practice, and live their lives based upon that freedom. The Left is not a fan of this freedom, they have made a push to move farther away from the fundamental beliefs that formed America. In many areas that once were benchmarks for displaying our major religious affiliation, we now see no religious connection at all.

1. Schools

2. Courthouses

3. Courtrooms

4. Government buildings

5. Businesses

6. Television programs

7. Holidays

Just to list a few, and the list is growing. In many cases, not just our religious connections, but any affiliation to the country itself is seen as offensive to the Left. No other area of our lives is under attack more however than our faith. There are many examples of faith becoming a target of the Left, and I will highlight some of those issues in this chapter. Before I get started, I want to be clear, not everyone on the

Left is calling for the canceling of faith, but there does exist a large number that want just that.

So, let's start with schools. Unless your child attends a private school, or a separate school board that is designed specifically to be Christian, or another faith, the religion aspect has been removed from the curriculum. Where I live there is an option to put your children in a Catholic or Public school, we chose Catholic. We chose Catholic because of the fact there is no religion taught in the public schools now. Once upon a time children stood for the national anthem, and Lord's Prayer, but they removed God from that morning routine. By removing the religious aspect of the children's teachings, we have allowed the schoolteachers, parents, and board itself to dictate more how the children are influenced. In many cases teachers from Kindergarten to University have made headlines for bringing their personal view to the forefront. We have seen Kindergarten teachers push gender issues without parental permission, and University professors belittle students for skin colour, and give preference to students of colour. We have also witnessed a change in important subjects. We have moved from math, reading, and writing skills to gender, and sexual orientation subjects. These issues are not typical subjects, but in today's world of being more inclusive, we are making room for them. Parents are not happy with some of the ways these new subjects are being introduced, and the Left are labelling them as Domestic Terrorists for their concerns. The main push to remove religion from public schools is cemented in the fear of offending other religions. I understand this to a degree, and including all religions would be incredibly hard. Removing faith entirely is not the answer either.

Parents should have a say in the subjects being taught to their children, and religion is one that should remain. My sons attend a Catholic school, and they don't just highlight Catholic values, but often have projects that has them research a wide range of religions and compare values systems. This open-minded approach allows students a chance to experience and observe other forms of religion as well. By removing all religious affiliations from the children's teachings, we remove a huge part of a system that will grow their strength, and values. By not allowing any religion to be taught, children are not being exposed to any faith building, which is what a large number of people on the Left want. Can any common ground be found on religious studies in school?

Once upon a time when you took the witness stand in a courtroom you swore an oath to be truthful by placing your left hand on the Bible and raising your right hand. It was something that signified that you would be truthful, and that God was your witness. They have removed the Bible, and just ask people to raise their hand and swear to be truthful now. So why did God have to be removed? Well, God was removed because today it is considered to be offensive to some who don't believe in God. Where we once considered God to be who we were witnessing before to keep us honest, we no longer allow Him into the courthouse or courtroom. We have removed the Holy witness and replaced Him with man's faith in ourselves. Our country was founded upon Christian faith, values, and our laws were created with the ten commandments in mind. The very laws that are upheld in court, but yet God is no longer allowed in. Government buildings are another place God has been removed. The very place that decided the laws of the Bible were the ones we would make laws over our country, have now turned-on God, and removed Him because His presence might offend someone that puts less value in faith, or in a different god.

Business is another area that freedom of religion has come into play. Offending those at work that are not religious can be as simple as having a Bible on your desk. The risk of offending someone has created a Public Relations and Human Resource nightmare. We have created an environment where we have removed all symbols of religion in order to appease the minority. Wearing a cross around your neck to work or school has been shunned or made a policy to alleviate the risk of offending others. I believe this is an infringement on our religious freedoms, all religions should be able to wear a symbol of their faith. Merry Christmas has been changed to Happy Holidays, changing Merry Christmas so that people that don't follow Christianity can join in the festivities without having to reference Christ, is not insulting to me as much as I find it to be slightly confusing. To join in a festivity to enjoy the gift giving, joy, peace and love, but not acknowledge the reason for those things is rather perplexing. The only answer I can think of is that the celebration, and magic of Christmas, enlightens us all, and if someone says to me Happy Holidays, I tell them Merry Christmas back. If you are offended by that, I will not apologize. A religious holiday or festival should not be expected to change because it is a better money maker for businesses. With the change from Christmas to Holidays, stores and businesses can encompass those that would otherwise not display those decorations or allow people to join in the tradition. A good debate topic, is it offensive, is it better to be inclusive, is it a Christian holiday? There are those people that say Christmas is a pagan holiday and that Jesus was born more in the spring, to that I say, we celebrate Christ, not the day, or the time of year.

Christmas is a great time of year, and the heavy shift towards the more inclusive Happy Holidays is only an infringement in my opinion if I have to stop saying Merry Christmas or have to take down any decorations with those words on them. The holiday today is designed to celebrate the birth of Jesus Christ, our Lord and Saviour, and if we are going to be forced to say Happy Holidays instead, that becomes the lack of religious freedom. I am all for celebrating cultures, festivals, and enjoying what other people bring to both Canada and the United States from around the world. Traditions are great things to share with friends, and communities we live in. Silencing our old traditions for new ones or silencing ours because someone is offended by them is something we must learn not to give into. Christians should not ask other faiths to change their celebrations to encompass us, and they should not do the same to us. I think we as a whole want to encompass other people's feelings, and feel we owe them a say. We must remember that our faith is what made North America a great democracy and brought a quality of life that brings people to our shores daily. To change who we are, or what we are allowed to worship would be to remove the fundamental right instilled upon the creation of our great nations.

Christmas has Santa Claus and Easter has the Easter Bunny. These two creations have become more important than Christ. With today's trend of less people attending church, or identifying as Christian, we will see Merry Christmas less and Happy Holidays more. In the last few years, we have witnessed cities removing ages old nativity scenes, Christmas trees in their squares, caroling, and houses being able to display decorations at the request of people that don't participate in celebrating Christ. Our religious freedoms should not tolerate removing our faith from our schools, Government, work, or anywhere else. One area that creates some challenge is when businesses give out a Christmas bonus, sometimes they will call it a winter bonus. These little changes are not offensive, we must try to find areas that help smooth tensions or could create problems but not remove freedom to worship Christ.

Of course, with any argument there exists challenges from opposing ideas. One argument could be made by those of different opinion than mine about people being able to refuse others based upon their religious beliefs. Case in point a baker refusing to make a cake for a same sex marriage. Your business is to bake treats for your customers. If those customers are a different religious, political, or sexual orientation than yourself, it makes no difference, your job is to make their order. I think it is very hard to stay to our faith, and yet be in the business world today, with changing values, and a disconnect with traditions. I think that in some cases, more than we probably know about, people are set up because of their faith. I feel that some people go out of their way to create an environment that they use to target people of faith. I personally have a Bible at work, I have it on my desk, and everyone in the mill knows I am a faithful person. I have not encountered anyone who has been offended or has asked me to put my Bible away. I feel this is a true testament to the people I work with, and to the type of person they are. I appreciate that they allow me that simple pleasure, and that they are not bothered by it at all.

The shows we watch have changed drastically from when I was young until today. I understand that new challenges are needed, and that different angles should be viewed, but a show that depicts Lucifer as the good angel and God's angels as the evil ones, is too far. It is blasphemous, and it is a slight against every Christian. The worst part is it is designed to do just that and attacking the main aspects of Christianity and twisting them is something only done to Christianity. No other religion has their value system mocked, or their premise twisted to offend them on purpose. There would be war if the Islam faith was attacked or their values mocked, and rightly so. Their defense of their religion is second to non, and they would not tolerate any attacks period. So, why is Christianity attacked openly by many in Hollywood, and on the Left? Why would Biden try and pass the Build Back Better bill and make churches exempt from receiving any funds for upgrades? Well, it would be speculation on my behalf, but faith is a strong glue that holds together those that believe, and I think that is the point under attack most. Hillary Clinton used the strong stance that Muslims defend their faith as a false motive for the Benghazi attacks that killed four American's. Clinton and Barack Obama had knowledge of an attack on the American embassy in Benghazi but failed to protect those men from harm, then after the attack, Clinton would ask what it matters if it was over a movie, or a terrorist attack. Well, it does matter because telling the truth, and owning up to your failure should be of utmost importance. Misleading Americans to believe it was not anyone's fault except a filmmaker attempting to alleviate her accountability in my opinion, is shameful.

The freedom to have a religion and to follow, and practice that religion is a great democratic right. Freedom of speech, and the ability to voice a dislike for others religious affiliation is also a right. Being faithful in today's world means that we have to be able to ignore others critical opinions, and to move on with our day. In the end, we can't be treated differently by our boss, or the Government, or by any business for our faith, so that is the freedom. Others around us don't affect how we walk in our faith, don't give them that power, or ability, and you will have a better day. In many cases, people that don't like the dedication it takes to follow faithfully behind a religion, will attack those that work hard at it. Sometimes, it is more about themselves than it is about you, or your religion.

We also must remember that our faith, and our beliefs are not those of everyone we encounter. No matter how dedicated to a religion you may be, you don't get to dictate that religion onto others. It really boils down to respect. We must respect each others individual rights, and freedoms, and embrace those things that are unique to us. I again highlight those fellow workers that respect my dedication to my faith and are unaffected by my choices. I, in turn don't go to work and demand that they participate in any of my religious practices, or engage in prayer, readings, or other things upon sitting with me during breaks. If the world was as respectful as my fellow workers on this aspect, we would be much better off.

I have always wondered about the affects of religion on medical procedures, and where the law and freedom of religion meet. Some religions are against blood transfusions, and any similar procedures, to the point of it causing death. Should a doctor have the right to save the life of a child whose parents refuse treatment? Does one's freedom to follow and practice a religion that forbids such treatment overrule medical necessity? I'm not sure a parent should have a say in this particular instance, but I also understand that faith dictates our path in life. Believing that something worldly can cause spiritual harm can have powerful affects on our decision making. Children under an age of understanding, or ability to make decisions for themselves are in their parents' care. And those parent's have the right to make all decisions regarding their wellbeing. I personally would stop at nothing to save my two sons from harm, and prayer would be top of my priorities.

"Religion has caused many wars on this planet", is an often-stated belief. It is untrue, not the religion itself mind you but those that follow them. War is caused by the failure of the people to be empathetic towards others, to be intolerant of others' beliefs, and values, to put less importance on life itself, than to set aside indifference. Religion is what people use as a scapegoat, a poorly concealed virtue signaling that there is no other course of action. We are at war to an extent with those people that want to vanquish religion from practice, and fellowship. People intent on the removal of religion from our lives. Some believing religion to be the cause of hate in the world, the cause of problems, and don't understand religious value. We must defend the rights, and freedoms of religion, or we will be told what values, and beliefs we are to follow.

Chapter Seventeen –

Freedom of Speech

As with freedom of religion, freedom of speech is a fundamental right enjoyed by everyone. Freedom of speech is under attack as much as freedom of religion is in my opinion. Today people don't like to hear opposing ideas, or different views of the same topic. Many people have become hyper focused on their views and anything different is considered offensive. In one incident a university professor once told Michael Knowles that his words were violence. Can you imagine, an opinion being aligned with violence? We have become so self absorbed that we can not be told something different from our own belief, or opinion, without feeling that we have been assaulted. Some people can not hear a different opinion without trying to cancel, silence, or in some cases have people arrested. One YouTube video showcased this best as a Left-leaning student called the police on a conservative reporter and crew to have them removed from campus. The police asked one simple question, "Did they assault you?" The student answered no to the question but wanted the police to remove them because he felt threatened by conservative ideas. And this is the most common attack on free speech today, the word, "threatened". To combat facts from those on the Right, the Left often goes to the same attempt, feeling threatened by the facts. In no situation should anyone feel that facts are somehow violence or threatening. It's absurdity to believe that your opinion is the only tolerable opinion allowed, or that your view on life is somehow the only view people can voice.

Universities are allowing conservative voices to be silenced, and when Donald Trump was President, he made a step towards changing this by withholding money to those Universities that did not address this wrongful action. Protesters at universities block the conference rooms used by groups whenever conservative groups book the room for use. If all groups are not allowed to have the same use of group rooms, why should they be eligible for Federal funding? Universities, where education, learning, and growth is the goal, should not promote the silencing of any side of the equation. I agreed with Trump's actions, and no school should want to paint targets on students for political beliefs. I feel that students begin to dabble in politics near the end of High School, and by university have begun to form their political affiliations, which usually leads to volunteering for candidates. And any action designed to punish, or to silence, and deter students from following, and socializing with other conservative minded students is shameful.

This action of silencing one political parties' ability to be heard on campus is closely aligned with communism and goes hand in hand with the new Left's socialistic trends. By making those students uncomfortable, or in some instances, with the use of violence, create an environment where conservative students feel they are under attack. These conservative minded students then arrange meetings off campus, to avoid fellow students' from blocking the use of group rooms. In many instances, even though off campus rooms are found to be used, those students opposed to conservative values, will show up and block the off-campus rooms as well. This behaviour needs to be changed, and Trump did just that, but universities need to combat this wrongful behaviour, and they should want to for the safety of all their students. There should be a portion dedicated to addressing this, and outlining how it will not be tolerated, during student induction to campus rules. And for a political party or it's supporters to be calling for unity out one side of their face, while advocating for silencing of all things Right, out of the other side, showcases nothing but hypocritical behaviour. It's called debating, and it's a lost aspect of conversating today, difference of opinion is what used to be the start of intelligent dialog. Communist countries use this same tactic to silence any free thought, or free idea, resulting in control over their subjects. This same tactic is what the Left is using, for the same desired outcome, power. They are starting in the schools, with Left leaning professors leading the charge against conservative students, designed to use labels to keep different ideas from being shared.

How harmful is having a different opinion?

1. Debates – open viewpoints

2. Dialog - creates abilities to voice your concerns.

3. Peak interest – listeners can become interested in joining.

4. Feelings – debate is not just about feelings; it must include facts.

5. Offended – if you are offended by other opinions, understand they are allowed to have one.

6. Silencing – an act of reducing the amount of information on any subject, because it is different than your own.

When teachers, or professors attack conservative students for their ideologies, or for their beliefs, it is important to address it. When a student in an American university writes his project centered on respect, on police officers, but is then demonized for his opinion by his professor, it's wrong. Teachers are to grade the project, not criticize the subject on which it is written, and use their own opinion to critique its value.

Another area that the Left uses to silence opposing ideas, and voices is through words. Labelling words to have ulterior meanings, other than their true meaning. Case in point when Governor Abbott from Texas called the millions of illegal immigrants flooding into the United States a surge and a crisis. He was attacked by some on the Left both in office and part of the news, for using the word surge. They then went on a rant trying to associate the word, "surge", with racism. This kind of behaviour is more of the same lies, and tricks to try and silence people from using words that truly describe the failures of the Left/Biden. Knowing that the facts speak for themselves and will be hard to counter argue that Biden's open border is a complete failure, they use tricks, and deceit to fool the uninformed. Words like surge, or MAGA, are not racist words, but yet the Left tries relentlessly to fool America that they are. When Trump first came out with Make America Great Again, the Left tried to tell American voters that this was Make America White Again, and tried to associate negative, hateful rhetoric in hopes of beating the Republicans. It didn't work, Trump won the 2016 election despite this underhanded attack. This style of word association would be present the entire Presidency of Trump and continues to be used on every Republican today by the Left supporting media. The media often uses negative words to describe the actions of Republicans, and often speak kindly of Democrats, this is a very useful tool. If the media, and the Democrats can work together to shift the viewpoint of the border crisis away from the failure of the Biden's Presidency, and focus on how the word, "surge", is somehow just Republicans being racist, the uninformed will believe it. There are many incidents similar to this one and was well used by Democrats like Adam Schiff during the Mueller Report and investigation.

You could not mention free speech and not mention the social media ban that Conservative voices are receiving. Donald Trump is banned from most social media platforms like Twitter, and Facebook, whereas others like Iranian dictators are free to talk about their hatred of Jewish people. Stacey Abrams refused to concede her race for Governor of Georgia to Brian Kemp and has continued to talk openly about how she feels she won that election. Hillary Clinton openly talks about how she beat Trump, and that she was the rightful winner of the Presidency back in 2016. So, when conservatives talk about the 2020 election, and the possibility that there was a rigged election, they are automatically banned from social media. The difference is, the social media is controlled by Left supporting CEOs, and they control what is talked about on their platforms. This is not free speech. If conservatives are unable to discuss topics without threat of ban, why are Left leaning users given total freedom. It is the single greatest election tool, control, and limit the Right while giving total access to the Left. If Elon Musk does buy Twitter, hopefully he opens his platform back up to those wrongly banned, and right this travesty of banning free speech for conservative voices.

Effects of the loss of free speech.

1. Ideas silenced.

2. One sided advantage during elections

3. If one side is silenced, then the Left will eventually turn on itself.

4. Leads to further chaos.

One of the greatest privileges of living in a free, and democratic country is the right to free speech. The ability to discuss and talk openly about all subjects. Today we see limits put on people depending on what political side of the aisle you are on. There's no shortage of examples of people being silenced, or cancelled, and this trend is very dangerous. Not because people are saying things that need to be stopped, but because people are unable to hear opposing ideas, and ideologies without labelling them as hate speech. I will discuss hate speech in a bit, however, opposing ideas to your Left leaning ones is not hate. I have watched videos of people trying to tell others that their facts about a subject is hate, and that is so baffling that we have lost reality and believe facts to be somehow hate. In many cases, the Left has a strong stance based on how they feel about a subject, whereas the Right usually comes in with the facts about that same subject. It is impossible to argue feelings with facts, and while I do agree that you should feel strongly about how our world is advancing, we must rely on factual based information more. This feelings over facts are what leads to the bans on social media, as people use the offended, and hurt feelings approach to call for silencing. Should we be so sensitive? Is there room for feelings in our discourse? I believe we must have feelings, we must be passionate about subjects, and we must be willing to debate these strong feelings. We can not be so led by our feelings though that we stop looking to find the facts that truly depict situations. We can not hide behind our feelings and never learn, grow or advance ourselves. I believe in the hierarchy of our growth, feelings are what starts us on a journey towards politics, sports, religion, or whatever topic. Feelings gets us hooked on a subject, and once we are enamoured with it, we look to understand it more, by searching for the facts. Once we have found the facts, we sometimes change our view about things. Many people I know have changed views about politics over the years, and change is inevitable, but informed change is critical.

By silencing one side and only allowing the Left a voice, how is that any different from communist countries? I recently ran into this same mindset at a bookstore near my hometown that would not allow my first book, Decency and Deception, Encouragement for a Struggling Nation on its shelves. The reason they won't bring in my book is simple, the owner supports the Democrats, and my book is a conservative based book. Don't they believe in giving their customers equal opportunity to purchase and read books from both sides? Well, the clear answer is no, they don't, and this is not the only place you will find this closed-minded approach. It is a closed-minded approach, and the biggest question is how can a nation come back together, heal, move forward, and better themselves with an approach that has failed every nation that has tried it?

I mentioned that the Left will attack itself if the Right is silenced eventually. We have witnessed this at times already, but their behaviour will not change and if they successfully silence the Right, they will then be forced to silence those among themselves that differ slightly. This will only create an environment of chaos, and will further create tolerance of a single ideology, which is in line with what the Bible preaches. So, is the attack on free speech Biblical? Well, some would believe that to be true, I encourage you the reader to do some research for yourselves. The one thing that we can all agree upon I would hope is that one side being given the right to free speech while the other is forbidden is wrong.

This leads us to something called Hate Speech.

abusive or threatening speech or writing that expresses prejudice against a particular group, especially on the basis of race, religion, or sexual orientation.

Hate speech is defined by the Cambridge Dictionary as "public speech that expresses hate or encourages violence towards a person or group based on something such as race, religion, sex, or sexual orientation!

In many cases today we see the Left describing facts as hate speech, or dialog between the Right and Left as hate speech because of the definition that states encouragement of violence. Hate speech is not the use of facts, and it is not the denial of pronouns. The Left tries to associate a difference of opinion, and the difference of belief in many aspects between Right and Left as violence, or threatening, and quite simply it is not. Hate speech is when groups of people are attacked, or the call to harm certain people based upon race, religion, sexual orientation, not by simply disagreeing with ideologies.

Some people argue that hate speech should be allowed because it falls under free speech. Social media uses hate speech as a pretense to silence people, but seem to only apply that to conservative users, and falsely might I add. Real hate speech is given the green light as Iran continues to use social media but calls for the death of Jewish people. It is a very debated subject between hate and free speech, what qualifies, and should social media be allowed, or compelled to control it. I agree that social media has a certain obligation to control what is said on their platforms but have also done a very poor job at masking their bias, in favour of the Left. Again, maybe if Elon Musk buys Twitter that maybe even the playing field a bit more.

Compelled Speech.

The compelled speech doctrine sets out the principle that the government cannot force an individual or group to support certain expression. Thus, the First Amendment not only limits the government from punishing a person for his speech, it also prevents the government from punishing a person for refusing to articulate, advocate, or adhere to the government's approved messages.

https://www.mtsu.edu/first-amendment/article/933/compelled-speech

This is what Dr. Jordan Peterson was making his stand against. Justin Trudeau legislated which words could be used, or more forcing people to use certain pronouns when it came to gender. The definition clearly describes that this was a clear infringement of our rights. Now Dr. Peterson himself has stated that it is not about the pronouns, but solely about the Government compelling us to use certain words and following it up with punishment if not adhered to. I feel that it is a clear infringement, and as more people choose to use different pronouns all the time, how does one keep them straight, and most I have never heard of before. It is not out of a lack of respect that I feel this is wrong of Trudeau, but it ultimately forces people to use words and to accept stances on gender that they may not agree with. This is clearly not the role of the Government, and I feel that it should not have passed into law.

Should words be legislated ever? I feel that by forcing people to use words, groups of words, or single words, it creates a rebellious atmosphere whereas people will more likely do the opposite. I also feel that governments should not force social movements on people through the use of power. If someone asks their friends to use certain pronouns, those friends will most likely use them. If those same people ask strangers to use certain pronouns, there is a chance that someone might disagree, and refuse. It all boils down to respect. Not just respecting those asking people to use pronouns but respecting the rights and freedoms of those that choose not to use them.

Free speech is not about being able to say anything, there should be laws that prevent hate from being spread. There also needs to be present guidelines for what hate speech is. In today's world, we don't use our vocal abilities like we once did. Most conversations today are online, on some form of social media. These social media sites have become incredibly important during elections, because the ability to reach people is so vast. Having a strong social media team during your campaign for any election, at any level is crucial. People tend to say things online that they otherwise would not feel comfortable saying face to face with someone. This creates a toxic environment sometimes, and the greatest potential for offense. There exist greater threats than that of what pronoun is used, on these social media platforms. Trump has been banned but it is not what he said more than it's great politically for those running against him. Creating a political advantage for one side is one area that governments should look into as far as regulating. If the likes of hateful dictators, from Russia, Iran, or any other country are allowed to use these platforms to spread their hate and lies, how could a former President be banned? If misinformation is the reason Trump is banned then the platforms are being hypocritical, because there is little to no fact checking of Left posts. The single greatest problem with getting your information online, and on social media is the accountability present. Every post that the Right makes, those are not banned, is hit with a fact check marker. This is another great tool of the social media owners to make it look less truthful, or to create what looks like false information. If Trump is banned over false information, why is the platform not addressing the rampant misinformation that is posted by others? The truth is, it's about control over how, when, and what is posted by the side the CEOs of the platform differ from.

No one should want to use hate speech; we are living in a time where we should all know better and be better. With all the information available to us, and at our fingertips, we should be far more concerned with how we impact those around us. Using pronouns that make people feel better, or more comfortable shouldn't be that offensive to anyone. At the same time, we shouldn't force people to use words that they are comfortable using or understand. Maybe if we took time to explain and listen to each other more our words wouldn't sound like hate to each other. Typical human behaviour, we have taken the greatest advantage known to mankind, the internet, and used it to hurt others. There will always exist those people that are hateful, petty, and mean, and just because they exist doesn't mean we have to give them the time of day. There are tools available to us for this. We can block people from platforms, we can block comments, we can unfriend, etc. But we should only do this if we use the same guidelines for everyone. Whether we are talking about free speech, hate speech or compelled speech, we should all remember one old saying.

"Hate corrodes the container it is carried in."

I once heard former Senator Al Simpson say this at the funeral of George H. W. Bush, and it couldn't be more true.

Chapter Eighteen –

Military Stance.

The military stance differs drastically from the Republican Party to the Democratic Party, and that is not necessarily a good thing. When the Republicans are in power, or in the White House, the world seems to take the President's remarks more seriously, and before you ask what I mean I will give examples.

1. Ronald Reagan – Iranian hostages

2. Donald Trump – Taliban

3. Donald Trump – Ukraine/Russia

4. Barack Obama – Syria

5. Bill Clinton – USS Cole

6. Barack Obama - Iran Nuke Deal

7. Ronald Reagan – Cold War

8. John F. Kennedy – Cuba Missile Deal

So, let's look at each of these eight situations listed above briefly, and highlight the differences. Now I realize that people that support the Democrat side will try and relate how being passive, or less aggressive is a better approach to conflict. I even understand that to be true, in some cases, but for the most part, letting the world know that poor treatment of people anywhere in the world will not be tolerated actually saves lives. This articulation of the American capabilities, and willingness to defend those that can not do so for themselves, is crucial to being proactive in defending life. This is something that can be debated, but for me in my lifetime, it is well documented. Weakness, constitutes aggression from those wicked, and maniacal leaders, wishing to ascertain control over others. I have followed politics since the early eighties, thanks to great teachers who asked our class to get involved in the world around us. So, having watched closely for all these years, I have formed a strong opinion on military use, and the need for its presence in the world. I do little to hide the fact that Ronald Reagan was my favourite President, and that his accomplishments were outstanding.

Let us first look at how Ronald Reagan, and the hostage situation that faced the world started. President Jimmy Carter had attempted to broker a deal that would see the hostages, fifty-two to be exact, released from Iran, but failed. During the campaign trail, Ronald Reagan, and Jimmy Carter had very intense debates, and unfortunately for Carter, he was knee deep in a hostage situation, and a campaign trail at the same time. While it was Jimmy Carter that brokered the deal to free the hostages, most believe on the Right anyways, that Ronald Reagan's threats to send the military in if those hostages were not released within so many hours of his taking the Oval Office. On his inauguration, the hostages were released. I personally believe that Carter was not being taken seriously by Iran, and that Iran had the upper hand. Reagan however, changed the entire plan, not by anything he did, but in WHO Iran was now dealing with. More likely to send military might to free hostages, or to get vengeance for those killed already. This was the difference, and there is no shortage of conspiracy theories about the situation, and how it ended. I won't get into those theories, although I do love to debate facts against them. Bottomline, Reagan's view of the military's capabilities, and the purpose of the military, was the deciding factor in those hostages being released. I do also realize that Jimmy Carter and his team of negotiators should not be totally discredited in the release of hostages. However, Carter's Presidency was in no way, shape, or form a success, and his team released millions of dollars to the Iranian Government to help secure the release. The hostages were held 444 days, Carter tried a military operation code named Operation Eagle Claw, which failed miserably. We witnessed the same political approach with Obama and the Syrian situation during his Presidency. Ronald Reagan did not negotiate with Iran that is a fact, but Jimmy Carter failed a few times to release the hostages, and only once he was removed from office did Iran finally release them. Whether it was Ronald Reagan's coming into power or Iran waiting until Jimmy Carter was out of power, Iran had the upper hand on Carter, and once that changed, Reagan inherited that success.

Donald Trump took over the office of the President of the United States and just like Reagan inherited a situation neglected or handled poorly by a Democrat President before them. Obama had allowed the Taliban to not only take a strangle hold of Syria but branched out causing destruction and chaos in the surrounding areas as well. Destroying ancient sites, and artifacts as they went. Murdering hostages, and anyone they felt necessary, and in inhumane fashion. At one point Obama referred to the Taliban as JV, or juvenile. Well, those JV warriors were not contained by Obama, and he failed to save the lives of many people. During Donald Trump's term in office there was hardly any Taliban or other like organizations reeking havoc around the world. And at one point Trump was nominated for the Nobel Peace Prize for his work at getting Iran and Israel to sit down together. Iran would walk away from that because Joe Biden took over office, and Iran had plans of returning to their Obama era nuke deal. Just having Trump in office seemed to quell the tension around the world. North Korea invited Trump to cross into their country, Taliban was silent, as were other terrorist groups. The only war waged against Trump was from the Democrats, and the media. Of course, the Taliban would come back strong under Biden, and take over Afghanistan in such a fashion that troops would have to be sent back in to rescue people. Sadly, 13 members of the military would lose their lives in the effort to save others from the coming terror of the Taliban. Biden's pullout of Afghanistan might be his biggest mistake to date, but there are so many to weigh it against that might be hard to prove. The fact remains that where Trump had the Taliban silent for his term in office, Biden was the cause of their return to power, and in devastating fashion.

Ukraine and Russia are no strangers to war. They are often at war with each other, and the President of the United States has some factor in this I believe. During Obama's time in office Russia invaded Ukraine and tensions were high. However, during Trump's time in office Russia was not actively at war with Ukraine. Enter Joe Biden to the White House, bam, Russia is back in the Ukraine. This is not merely coincidence; this is due to the weak military stance of Democrat Presidents. Joe Biden on the campaign trail even bragged that Putin knows how he operates and that he doesn't want to deal with him. Well Joe, he doesn't seem to think much of your power, he wasted little time going back to war under your watch. When Obama was President, Biden was video taped telling a crowd how he refused to give Ukraine aide money until his son Hunter was saved from prosecution, and yet zero actions were taken against him for this. Trump, however, was impeached by the Democrats for making a call to Ukraine to see if they were at all looking into this situation. Two totally different approaches to the same conflict, and sadly that conflict continues to fester today. My hope is that peace, and safety for everyone can be found soon.

During Barack Obama's time in office Syria was in civil war. Obama had given them a red line, or a line in the sand so to speak. Obama tried to influence the war but did little to change anything from happening. The war waged on and then branched out into surrounding countries. As people around the world watched in horror as people were beheaded, and killed in the most inhumane ways, Obama called them JV, or juvenile. They were anything but, and many, many lives were affected by this weak effort from Obama. People from many different countries were going over to join the terror groups causing chaos in the area. It was almost like they saw it as an opportunity to be part of history. Then once they spent time over there, they wanted to be welcomed back home with open arms. Britain and Canada had many people return, and it was met with distain by everyday citizens who felt these were monsters returning. Most people felt they should be in jail not welcomed back to taxpayer dollar rehabilitation for becoming indoctrinated by these hate groups. In Canada, a few well known returning recruits received payouts of money from the government, which taxpayers were enraged by. My personal feelings about this are simple. If you decide to leave Canada, United States, or any country to fight in a war like the one in Syria, and commit heinous acts, you have forfeited your right to citizenship in those countries you left. You wanted to be part of the Syrian civil war; you now belong to Syria. Let the debate on citizenship begin. Should you be able to lose your citizenship? Should you be allowed to behave like terrorists and be allowed back home without prosecution? Well, that is not up to me, but I feel that it should be something well researched before people are allowed to return to normal life after such actions.

One Democrat decision made without our Allies Israel's best wishes was Obama's decision to give Iran nuclear capabilities. The Iran Nuke Deal as it is mostly known by, gives America very little if any chances to inspect the sites where the plutonium is being used, and very little chance of knowing if missiles are being made. Iran has voiced a distain for Israel and has voiced a want to wipe them from the face of the earth. So, to allow them the capacity to potentially create nuclear weapons is absurd. During Obama's time in office Iran was not a well-behaved country, and when Trump followed Obama, taking over the White House, he cancelled the Iran Nuke Deal. However, true to form, Biden returning to Obama2.0 politics, has again opened talks of returning to the deal. And if Biden doesn't have the House and Senate to back his agenda, he will perhaps use Executive Powers to try and accomplish this. Israel has voiced its opinion very loudly that if Iran were to produce nuclear warheads, Israel would be their intended target. Donald Trump understood this, even worked with Benjamin Netanyahu to move the US embassy to Jerusalem, and to cancel the Iran Nuke Deal.

The attack on the USS Cole in October 2000 while it was in Yemen, ended the lives of 17 servicemembers lives, and injured 40 others. This attack was carried out by Al-Qaeda and Osama Bin Laden even took credit for the attack. A suicide bomber boat came up beside the guided missile destroyer and detonated itself ripping a 40ft wide hole in the side of the USS Cole. The USA sent over hundreds of FBI antiterrorist department and found two men guilty. The men would later be killed by the US in targeted attacks, but some among the United States thought more should have been done to hold Yemen and Al-Qaeda accountable. I personally believe that the USS Cole attack was a gauging Al-Qaeda used to test how readily the USA was to launch an attack. I also believe that had President Clinton done anything to hold these people accountable the 9/11 attack on the world trade towers would not have happened. This is a very debatable subject, but had the attackers been engaged by the US forces they would not have had the time to plan and execute these attacks. Obviously, Al-Qaeda was looking for a fight, and when they didn't get one, they made their stance more pronounced. Bill Clinton would do an interview with Chris Wallace that became heated as Wallace would ask questions about if Clinton did enough after the attacks. The interview was viewed as a Conservative hit piece by Clinton, and in the end stated he had not done enough to get Bin Laden after the attacks, but he tried. Clinton would state that Bush had eight months to do something after the end of Clinton's Presidency but chose to do nothing. Showcasing that Clinton is still upset by the overall view that he took a weak stance on the attack. Bin Laden was said to have been quoted in a book, The Tower, and it talks about how the fact that when you pulled troops out of Somalia in 1993, bin Laden said, "I have seen the frailty and the weakness and the cowardice of U.S. troops."

https://www.foxnews.com/video/1178586625001

I'm quite sure that Clinton did not hold Bin Laden accountable, and that he could have done far more to prevent more loss of life. I am also sure that twisting the points of the situation to make the next President look bad because of your own failure is not a point to brag about. To get mad at Chris Wallace, and to use the phrase, "but I tried", only makes you look like how Bin Laden said you look, weak. I feel that Clinton's anger was a clear signal that he knows he failed, but I also feel that maybe he is partially right about the Bush administration not taking Bin Laden seriously enough either. You could never have guessed that the 9/11 attacks would transpire, or that the USS Cole would be attacked. It is easy for me to criticize Bill Clinton for his role, and to play armchair quarterback, but the fact that he remains so angry about the mere question of his role, makes me believe he could most definitely have done more. Perhaps, like I said earlier, the view Bin Laden, and Al-Qaeda had at the time of the US military led to the attacks on the World Trade Towers. Where I believe that Clinton is as much to blame for the attacks as Bush is, maybe even more so.

Let's now move to a different President, and one that was not viewed as a weak, or slow to respond. Ronald Reagan would engage in a different type of war, one that would see proxy wars fought, but no real regional war. The Russians and the United States the obvious largest contributors to this war. The timeline of the start, and the full extent of the Cold War is debated among many, but the fact remains that Reagan ended it. He obviously worked with Mikhail Gorbachev, President of the Soviet Union. I remember the two men having a respect for each other, for the lives of the people in their countries, and for peace. It would not have been accomplished had not both men been so strong and viewed as equals. If one had been viewed as weak, or incapable of leading their side, who knows the Cold War might still be going on. There was no shortage of strong leadership on both sides over the span of the Cold Wars life. Most agree that it started shortly after WWII, and with many conflicts waged in proxy battles. Some have said that Ronald Reagan won a war without a single bullet fired, this is not entirely accurate, he out bought the Russians, and ultimately won the right to tell Gorbachev to tear down this wall in Berlin. Did Reagan win a war without a single bullet being fired? Yes, and no, he won without WWIII starting, and without any invasion, but in those proxy wars some shots were fired. I first became interested in politics because of Ronald Reagan and Mikhail Gorbachev, because of their humanity, and dedication to life. To making the right decision over the one held over time. We have lost both of these men now, and I wish I could have sat and talked with both men. War is ugly, but the end of the Cold War was a win for almost all involved. Weakness would not have accomplished this great task.

The Cuban Missile Crisis was the closest the Cold War came to full scale war. The Russians were believed to be transporting nuclear weapons to Cuba to prevent further invasion threats after the failed Bay of Pigs invasion. Planes used to take pictures of Cuba, captured clear launch sites and President Kennedy would be tested over a course of days before Russian ships would eventually turn around. I believe that because of the weak view Kennedy had after the Bay of Pigs failure, the Russians were ripe to test him, and would have been in great striking distance of the United States had he not been firm over the Cuban Missile Crisis. Reagan would be asked in his debate with Walter Mondale if he, at his advanced age could have put in the long hours needed to accomplish this win. His answer was the very point that won him the debate and White House. His answer was,

Reagan's answer was, "Not at all, Mr. Trewhitt and I want you to know that also I will not make age an issue of this campaign. I am not going to exploit for political purposes my opponent's youth and inexperience.

https://www.nytimes.com/1984/10/22/us/the-candidates-debate-transcript-of-the-reagan-mondale-debate-on-foreign-policy.html

Had the Russians sensed fear on the behalf of the USA, war would most definitely broke out. Kennedy gets a win, and his popularity would be like nothing any President has seen. Sadly, he would be shot and killed, assassinated in Dallas, Texas. JFK and his brother Robert Kennedy would both meet this same end. Their lives cut short, their work unfinished, and the countless great things that they might have accomplished, silenced. In short order JFK, Robert Kennedy, and MLK would all be assassinated, maybe one of the biggest losses one single country could face, over five years. Robert Kennedy would announce Martin Luther King Jr.'s death at an event in April, but he would be killed that same year in June.

One example of weakness would be Joe Biden's pulling out military troops from Afghanistan without better planning, only to have to return try and save hundreds of lives stuck at the airport. He openly bragged that the Taliban would not retake the country swiftly, and that it would not be like how the US left Vietnam, on rooftops with helicopters. Well, both of those things Joe got wrong. Of course, Biden would blame Trump for the pull out, and he would blame Trump for the failure. The truth of the matter is that Trump promised to pull the troops out by a date, and Biden had months to do so, but waited until it was too late to do so properly. Biden ended up pulling the troops out before the civilians that worked for/with the US troops. Leaving these people behind to fend for themselves, and with so much military equipment abandoned, it was a complete failure on the Biden administration. Thousands of people were stuck at the airport in Kabul, so many that the US had to send troops back to help. How could Biden feel leaving these people behind was at all the right thing to do? The Taliban would end up bombing the airport, and thirteen servicemen/women would lose their lives in these attacks. The Taliban knew that Biden was weak, and that it was the best time to take over the country again. The current government that was in place gone in an instant, replaced by the Taliban, who were now better equipped with military equipment than ever. So dire was the situation, people were clinging to aircrafts as they took off, and falling to their death. After this botched operation, Russia went into the Ukraine, an act of aggression, the last time Russia did this was when Biden was Vice-President under Barack Obama. China has threatened to forcibly take over Taiwan, and North Korea has threatened South Korea with nuclear strikes.

Once you project a view of weakness to the world, the behaviours of the world leaders react to that image.

The biggest difference between the Democrats and Republicans when it comes to the military is perhaps spending. The Republicans believe investing in the military is crucial, that training, and new equipment will save lives. Often the Democrats cut spending to the military, and the end result is a need later to invest again. The willingness to send troops in to help other countries might be something that both Parties share evenly. The role once the troops get there might be different, but the world relies on the United States to be the righter of wrongs. A presence of power, strength, and to uphold freedom. When Ronald Reagan took office, he might not have brokered any deal with Iran to free hostages, but Iran knew he would send large scale military action their way, and they wanted no part of it. My opinion, based on what I've witnessed over the last forty years has been that Republicans in the White House see less aggression from the malevolent, where the Democrats are entangled in aggression.

Now to say such a thing I would be amiss if I didn't provide some examples.

1. Ronald Reagan – Cold War end, Iran hostage ended,

2. George H. W. Bush – ended Iraq in Kuwait

3. George W. Bush – Iraq war, 9/11 attack.

4. Donald Trump – Taliban, Al-Qaeda, North Korea, Iran silenced.

5. Bill Clinton – USS Cole, Bin Laden emboldened by weakness to plan 9/11

6. Barack Obama – Russia invades Ukraine, Taliban, Al-Qaeda, Syria, Benghazi, ISIS

7. Joe Biden – Russia invades Ukraine again, Taliban takes Afghanistan.

The United States under either watch, Republican or Democrat use the military to help others around the world. It is a great service to the betterment of the world, and to helping those unable to defend themselves. You may not agree with my points as to the difference a President can make, but when needed the Republicans become the aggressor more often. And Democrat Presidents are usually tested far more often by the malevolent. Donald Trump looking at the military, especially the Navy, and their patrolling the waters of Japan without Japan paying the bill was an interesting twist. If a country receives help should there be a cost associated to them for that? I would love to hear a good debate on that.

Chapter Nineteen –

House and Senate

For any President to have an easy time getting his agenda passed into law, he must have the power of both Senate and House representatives, working for him/her. If the President doesn't have the backing of either, by majority he/she will have a very difficult time getting things accomplished. To keep any President from passing bad bills, agendas, or spending, it is ideally better for Americans if each Party has the majority of one. This forces both parties to work together, or compromise on situations, with the taxpayer coming out ahead, instead of just paying the bill.

If the President loses the majority of both House and Senate, the voters have sent a clear message to the President to work on better things, as the House and Senate can change every two years. By having midterm elections, the American voters have the power to change the ability a President has to making decisions, by giving, or taking away majority rule. This would leave the President no other means than to use Executive Order or work with the House and Senate to make better decisions. Joe Biden, in his first term as President, and hopefully only, faced strong House and Senate change. Currently as I am writing this book the election has just concluded. The new way elections are held in the USA takes the better part of a week to get 100% of the results. This baffles me as the elections are mostly electronic from what I gather, and do not understand how it could take days to count the results. As of right now the House is 201

Democrat to 211 Republican with 218 being the magic number for majority, and the Senate is tied at 49 seats with 51 being the magic number. Either way, if the Democrats hold off losing both Senate and House or even just losing one, voters are clearly not happy with Biden's decisions. With the numbers being so close to majority for both sides America is not overwhelmed with either Parties views, but Biden has lost the overall faith of the voters.

To win the voters over during the 2022 midterm elections Biden offered to pay off student loans. This was not sent to the House and Senate and was passed by Executive Order. Only two days after the midterms were over, a Federal Court overturned the student loan forgiveness, and critics started to react to this by calling it a midterm election strategy. Obama worked to help the Democrats, by campaigning, Bill Clinton, Hillary Clinton, all worked to sell what Joe Biden has done as a good thing. It clearly was not being bought by voters, as the election is still in limbo. It was Democrat majority before midterms and is only theirs to lose. This is the power of the people at work, and the people have spoken with less faith in Biden even if he keeps both in the end, he has barely held onto, and maybe lose both.

So why is having majority important? Well, if Donald Trump didn't have majority of the Senate during his Presidency, he would have been impeached and removed from office by Democrats, and on things not worthy of removal. The Democrats worked tirelessly on the Mueller report, only to have it fall flat, but were hoping to remove Trump from office. It did not happen, so Trump was impeached over a call to Ukraine's President that the Democrats decided was abuse of power. The Senate was Republican majority and found him not guilty. The House was Democrat majority and found him guilty. When Joe Biden was Vice President, he withheld $1B of aide money to the Ukraine unless they fired the prosecutor that was looking into Hunter Biden dealings in the Ukraine. This somehow, was not worthy of any actions from the Democrats or Republicans but making a phone call was. If the Republicans didn't have majority rule

Trump would have been removed from office, and the shame would have been squarely on the Democrats for using their power wrongly to overthrow a President that had done nothing wrong. Should not a President ask question of such a situation? I feel more should be done to Biden for this admission on video of withholding aide until his son was cleared of investigation. If Hunter had done nothing wrong, what is the problem with a simple check of his dealings?

Trump was again impeached by the House Democrats for the January 6 Capital building riot. This would have been the first time a President would be impeached after leaving office. He would not be found guilty again by the Senate. The role of the House and Senate is not, I repeat not to impeach Presidents over any and every action taken, but for abuse of power where they personally gain from it. Closer to what Biden did by saving Hunter Biden from prosecution by withholding money needed and promised to an Ally. The fact that Nancy Pelosi would brag about Trump forever being impeached and smiling like it was a real accomplishment shows that the reality of how embarrassing this move was, is lost on her and her colleagues. Can American voters count on House Democrats and Senate Democrats using the impeachment route every time they gain majority if the President is Republican? Does the impeachment ability need to be made more specific so it can't be used to remove a President elected by the voters, by underhanded means? I believe that it would have made a laughingstock of the Democrat Party had they removed Trump, and that they tried it twice shows they will continue to try anything.

What are some of the things Democrats worked on other than impeachment.

1. Questioning Candace Owens about white supremacy

2. Questioning Judge Kavanaugh with guilty verdict mentality

3. Questioning Judge Amy Coney Barrett's ability to pass judgement (faith)

4. Spending absurd amounts of money causing inflation to be 40yr high

5. Maxine Waters calling for longer protests.

6. Border denial

Let's first look at Candace Owens, and the way she was questioned by a joint committee. She was questioned about the threat of white supremacy being a huge threat to blacks in America. She was first told she should be ashamed of herself by another guest speaker, a white woman who misrepresented her previous answer on the subject. Then she was played a small audio of an answer she gave without proper context, or the question she was originally asked. She dealt with each situation amazingly, first to the woman guest speaker she clarified the deception attempt, then asked if we are not above such low behaviour. Perfect answer, and response putting the appropriate shame on the correct person. Then she clarified to a shocked Democrat Senator who also attempted to mislead by his audio, that he should also be ashamed for his attempt to twist information to fit his narrative. Then she closed with a very clever observation about an all-white guest speaker panel, pressing her on white supremacy as she is a black woman. I believe the rational behind this absurd questioning was to try and discredit one of the absolute smartest, and most intelligent minds coming along on the Republican side. Candace Owens is as smart as she is beautiful, and that is a threat to the Democrat side, who usually use race issues to their advantage. Candace Owens could quite possibly be President someday soon. If in 2024 Donald Trump is looking for a Vice running mate, he should consider Candace Owens.

The way Judge Kavanaugh was questioned about allegations of sexual misconduct was where Democrats went wrong in their proceedings. Whenever allegations of misconduct arise the House and Senate should be given ample time to question the person being accused. I believe that is a key role of being an elected official. Judge Brett Kavanaugh was not given a fair questioning in my opinion and was treated with disgust. Many on the Democrat side treated Kavanaugh as though he were guilty before hearing the information, and answers he had to give. Protesters were ever present in the street with professional signage that someone had to have paid for, protesters usually make their own signs with cardboard and markers, not order professional signs. So why the theatrics? Both Ford and Kavanaugh should have had fair, and non bias stances before joint committee questioning, and the truth will be found. I'm not saying anyone was guilty or innocent, but if I was questioned in such a way, that I was already guilty, I would be upset and angry at Democrats. At the same time as the Kavanaugh questioning a Democrat Keith Ellison was being accused of misbehaviour by an ex-girlfriend, but it fell on deaf ears to those supporting Ford and her accusations.

Likewise, Amy Coney Barrett was questioned before joint committee and her performance as a judge was put to the test, but more so her Christian faith. Both Kavanaugh and Barrett would have their families brought into the mud slinging and that is unfair, un-American, and appalling. I understand that Trump was filling the Supreme Court vacancies, and that the Democrats want those positions filled with people who are loyal to the Democrat side, and that Roe vs Wade was at stake. But the questioning was beyond obtrusive if you ask me. Amy would be asked by Hawaiian Democrat if she has ever sexually assaulted anyone, which was about as crazy a question, and waste of time as you get. This associating all things negative with the Right or Republican is getting out of hand and causing the Left to embarrass themselves.

I will say it again, people that are accused of wrongful behaviour should answer to those allegations, but they should be innocent until proven guilty just like they should be in court. Just because it isn't an actual court shouldn't allow those sitting on the committee to act out their own bias and we should expect better out of people elected by the people for the people.

Not to rewrite all the same things I have already covered in the chapter on inflation, but the House and Senate have as much fault as Biden does for passing the spending amounts. Due directly to the spending of the Biden administration and backed by the Democrats in both the House and Senate inflation is at a 40year high. Even though both Biden and his colleagues in the House and Senate continue to claim that it costs nothing to spend the money, and Biden even went so far as to say he cut the national debt in half, it doesn't make the statements true. The truth is that government spending is the biggest cause of inflation. Biden and his colleagues also continue to claim inflation is caused by Russia/Ukraine conflict. And, again Biden and his administration have spent way more money on Ukraine than they have on the southern border where that issue continues to fester, without answer. The money spent on Ukraine is commendable, however, if they spent it on closing the border, finishing the much-needed wall, it would have built up infrastructure at the same time.

The Build Back Better would have increased the debt even further but was held back by Democrat Joe Manchin. The original cost was a $3.5 trillion package including provisions related to climate change and social policy. It was negotiated down to $1.7 trillion and was passed in the House Nov 19,21. It was renegotiated to become the Inflation Reduction Act of 2022, which is ironic as it will cause more inflation than it will reduce. But if you call it the Inflation Reduction Act people will believe it. Again, I will say that Build Back Better, was designed to reward those cities that set themselves on fire for the leadup to the 2020 election, and Biden's administration had zero plans of the money going to help build, or unify the people because strangely enough, churches were exempt from receiving the money. Why would places of worship, those very places that saw police shut down services in parking lots, be exempt? The real funny part is movies were still made, and parking lots in California were set up with huge tents for dining areas but going to stand in a parking lot for one hour to praise God, constituted the police shut it down.

Those members of the House and Senate should be upstanding people, they should strive for the betterment of their ridings, or constituents. This is not always the case, and it's hard to watch. Maxine Waters House representative for California's 43rd district was front and center at the Derek Chauvin verdict reading. She was out on the street telling protesters to, ""stay on the street" and "get more confrontational" if former Minneapolis police officer Derek Chauvin is acquitted in the killing of George Floyd. Now this is clearly inciting violence, at a time where riots and looting had plagued the US leading up to Biden taking office, to have a House Rep tell people to not go home, or trust the courts system, but rather get more confrontational, at the police officers' safety I might add. This should have been enough for every news channel to condemn her behaviour and ask her to step down. That was not the case, and in fact many news channels came to her defence, calling her an icon, and defending her statements. Now stop and think if this was a Republican House Rep., and we all know it would have been all the news reported, and the calls would be endless for that Rep. to step down. What if Chauvin had been found innocent? Would the lives of those officers, and jury members been safe? Would the potential injuries be on Waters head for inciting the violence? The answer is yes whether the verdict was innocent or guilty Waters clearly called for the incitement of violence, and in a city already on high alert Waters added gas to the fire. She should have been made to step down.

I have already detailed immigration, but I need to clarify how the House and Senate has handled the border situation. Under Trump AOC went down to highlight a broken system that she and her fellow Left Wingers called, "kids in cages", and "concentration camps". What she really did was theatrics and was designed to make Trump look evil by pretending that people who choose to enter a country illegally are not the ones responsible but Trump. All AOC accomplished was a need for a border wall, and that hypocrisy is alive and well inside the Democrat House and Senate. Biden's border is in absolute chaos, and where is AOC, and her movie crew? Where is the anguish AOC felt that doubled her over in pain for pictures at the site? Well, Biden's border is incredibly worse than Trump's, and it is ignored by House and Senate Democrats, as well as the news mostly.

The border agents targeted by the Biden administration really showcased to me anyways, that truth is far from the equation, and that everything is not as it seems. Border Agents took matters into their own hands and started to use horses to combat the illegal migrants crossing into the USA and were seeing great success with this approach. What did the Biden administration do to help them? Well, they made them stop using the horses, on what grounds you might ask. Well, nothing that was actually happening, but accused the agents of whipping the migrants, and forces them to stop using horses. Well, that should be easy to rectify, quick investigation, see that no whips were used, go back to using horses. The horses were working, and it didn't come from the Biden team, so it had to be stopped. This is why there is no unity in the USA, people's lives aren't the most important aspect, but perception is. There were no whips used by border agents, and even after it was proven, there was no apology from those that perpetrated this story. Where are the members of the Democrat House and Senate that actually care about the lives of both migrants, and border agents? Where are those members that want to visit the absolute chaos that has incredibly increased, under their President? And where are those members of House and Senate that saw fit to make the border a huge deal, voted against the wall being finished? I had a discussion not long ago with a friend that agreed the border was a disaster but didn't know how it could be fixed. My answer, "a wall". The answer was so right that zero response was given to it, and we both knew that wall should have been finished long ago.

Why Biden and his team would work so hard to spread a narrative that made hard working agents look like they are the problem instead of their own policies is shameful. As of November of

2022, to fill the holes in the border wall, container ship cargo containers have been placed two high, forming a makeshift wall. Sadly, the Democrats have been working harder at getting those containers removed than fixing the problem. You would think that House and Senate Democrats along with Republicans would want to secure that border, especially seeing how out of control the crossings have gotten. Numerous Republicans have called for the Biden team to do something, and Ted Cruz even tried to get a camera crew inside to see how things have progressed under Biden. He was not allowed in, because we all know, things have NOT progressed at all under Biden, but like I said earlier, gotten worse.

The role of the House and Senate is to work together to bring about laws and policies that better the lives of those people who elected you to do so. Not to work on impeaching Presidents so you can be petty and small. Working hard to create a better America than you started with or create bills to build up much needed areas of the country who are struggling. The job could not be more important than it is today. Unity is a word used by Biden when he took over the Oval Office but has become just another failed campaign promise. There needs to be a better working environment in Washington. There needs to be less meetings where we bring in people, browbeat them with small clips of things they have said, twisted to fit narratives that get exposed instantly, and tried again, and again in hopes of one sticking.

President Biden has failed in my opinion to change anything for the better since he took office. He has managed to create chaos or allowed others to create chaos around the world. He has had plenty of help along the way from his House and Senate Democrats. The border is in chaos, his economy, his inflation, his image around the world, and his ignoring these aspects, and saying he has done great things is scary to say the least. The amount of money passed since Biden has taken office will be the burden of future American's, and many of his colleagues want to spend even more.

Biden and his fellow Democrats want to add more seats to the Supreme Court of the United States, because they don't have the majority. The SCOTUS isn't an extension of the Republican or Democrat Parties. People nominated to serve on the SCOTUS should be chosen because they deserve to be there.

Chapter Twenty -

Supreme Court of the United States

One of the things going around the news today is how the Supreme Court of the United States is Conservative majority, and that the Democrats under Joe Biden, want to stack the SCOTUS. So, for one thing the law is not Republican or Democrat, and the Judges that sit on the SCOTUS do not make decisions based on what party they vote for. So, the entire notion of stacking the court to tip the scales of justice to give Democrats the advantage should be terrifying. It makes me ask myself, "what are they trying to pass that requires specific judges"?

To unpack the notion that Biden would need to stack the deck in his favour means he plans to pass things that special interest groups want passed that wouldn't stand a chance under normal circumstances. I'm not saying this is true, I'm just trying to wrap my head around why Biden would want to stack the court. A list of potential reasons I have thought of are as follows.

1. Abortion
2. Illegal migrants' citizenship
3. Voting without identification
4. Gun control

5. Censorship

6. Disinformation Board overreach

7. Education (ie. CRT)

8. Gender Affirming health care.

9. Gender in general

10. Mar-A-Lago like raids

The main difference between the two Parties today is clearly their views on what people are calling, "woke", issues. Not just these new issues, but also some ago old differences still exist between Democrats and Republicans.

The issue of women's rights, and namely abortion rights is a heavily controversial subject. My personal stance is that of Pro-Life, but obviously there are circumstances that I feel the option should be left open for. Democrats were worried about the possibility of Roe. Vs. Wade being overturned, and it was by the SCOTUS. This gives the power to the Governors of each State to make the law according to what each States voters want. This actually gives more power to the voters in each State and should be seen as a good thing. Companies are offering to pay for employee's abortions if they have to travel out of State to receive this procedure. One problem I have with the argument that the Left uses most often is abortion needs to be offered because of rape and incest. That particular aspect makes up less than 1 percent of all abortions. To further highlight this since Roe. V. Wade was passed in 1973, there have been approximately 63 million abortions performed. Which means in cases of incest and rape, approximately, 630 000 abortions that fall under the main argument for why abortion is necessary. I'm not saying anything other than the numbers, all views aside, just for that particular argument, less that 650 000 incest and rape related abortions were performed, over an almost 50year timeline. Of course, these numbers are not always agreed upon, but most people agree that it is low percentage for this argument. And I feel because of this low percentage for incest and rape those people on the Pro-Life side of the equation feel that the majority of abortions are performed for far less reasons, like as a form of birth control. I am not saying that I agree, or disagree with this, but I personally feel that this low percentage is why most are for life.

We are in a completely different world than the one we were when Roe. Vs. Wade was passed by the SCOTUS back in 1973. We have far greater technology, and we have gained so much by way of health care. We have things in our life that constantly change, and we don't always hold the cards on how and when they change. People choose to have abortions for many different reasons, and whether I agree with that choice or not, I understand that people have opposite opinions and are justified in their views. It is a very controversial subject, and one that is not easily navigated. A lot of very difficult decisions go into having an abortion, and it affects everyone differently.

Abortion also shifts into women's rights over men's rights, and the whole, "my body, my choice". There have been people asking the question if the woman gets to decide, do I get to opt out of paying if she keeps a child I didn't want. The answer is no, absolutely not. The reason is simply because you were happy to have sex, and you know that there exists a chance that a child can be conceived. If you get a woman pregnant and you become a father, you haven't lost money you have gained the most valuable thing on earth, treasure it.

Illegal migrants flooding into the country through the out-of-control southern border, are possibly being given citizenship by this Democrat Party under Joe Biden. Over the years, millions of people have come to America, and worked incredibly hard to obtain their citizenship, and become part of the "Melting Pot", that is America. This is not done overnight, or by running across an open field and into a political game that the media, and the Democrats are just not talking about. At one point the White House Press Secretary, Karine Jean-Pierre, made a statement that people weren't just walking across the border. Well, actually Karine, that is exactly what they are doing. And the Government you currently speak for daily is wanting them to become citizens without question. And not only is this the wrong way to handle or address the problematic border, at one point Biden was contemplating giving absurd amounts of money to each person crossing the border. There would have been Hell to pay for taxpayer's money going to illegal migrants, for entering the country and breaking the law. What people don't understand is that this act is actually illegal, and the people need to be deterred from entering, not encouraged like Biden is doing.

The other main problem with Biden's open border is the fact that Democrats are fighting to have people voter without having to show identification. In order to vote in the United States, you should most definitely have to produce picture identification, proving you are able to cast a vote in the election. You can't drive a car without picture id, you can't buy alcohol without showing your id, you can't even get into club membership sites without your club card. If these things need the simple act of producing id, then casting votes to select the Governor, Senator, House Rep and President all are totally deserving of such an act. The fact that the Democrats are trying to push such a thing calls into question what on earth for? If they control the SCOTUS, then they would have a good chance of getting this passed. If Biden simply makes open chairs to fill with Democrat selected judges, I feel it might muddy the water a bit, creating a more political environment than one based on the law. Which is why it is being talked about by the Democrats in the first place, and not because there aren't enough judges to handle the workload currently, but to push a certain agenda. Not once has the workload been mentioned, so clearly it is agenda driven, and that is unconstitutional, for either Party to try and persuade a judicial system. It should never be allowed, period.

Now another highly controversial subject is gun control. Biden passing assault weapon bans after even more shootings at universities will be met with agreement and distain. In places like Texas where a great number of people carry weapons, violent crimes are much lower than in areas such as Illinois, specifically Chicago. I am a big believer that if you take the guns out of law-abiding citizens it will give the criminals the advantage. As the criminals will be the only ones armed. Taking the guns might not be the right approach, but there is however, much needed work to be done on how accessible guns are, especially to those with mental illness. To use a stacked SCOTUS to get a Democrat viewpoint passed on gun control will not end well, and gun owners will not stand for such action. The second amendment gives American's the right to keep and bear arms. As a Canadian myself, we have much more strict gun laws than the United States, and therefore we see far less gun related crimes. We also have far less population numbers. Among the people in Canada that are hunters, I would say that the gun numbers would be relatively close. Where we differ, the most is handguns, and the ability to carry them. We simply can not unless it is for work, or trapping. I do not feel that the violence in America is due to law abiding people having guns, rather those that choose to use them to harm others, showcasing a need for background checks, and a federal card like the Canadian Possession and Acquisition License. It does not limit your rights, or number of guns allowed, but it does limit who can possess weapons. Now, you will never change the criminal element from obtaining illegal guns, or what they do with those illegal guns, but it will be a start, a much-needed start. Using the SCOTUS to ban assault weapon's is also controversial because aren't all guns, assault weapons? The definition is what trips up some people on the Right. And just because a weapon is black in colour doesn't make it any more of an assault style weapon. The gun control issue is going to be a much-debated topic for years to come, and if any one subject could possibly bring the two sides together to talk it should be guns.

To everyone who has lost a loved one due to gun violence my heart aches for your loss. Especially if it was a child in a school. Gun violence needs to end, period!!!!

When it comes to censorship, and we have witnessed a great deal of censorship on the side of the Right over the last few years. Twitter banning Donald Trump, and the majority of people who discuss the 2020 election if they feel the coincidences of some things that happened election day night don't add up, are instantly banned from all social media platforms. I myself had a video taken down from my YouTube account because I discussed election day happenings. So, why ban people on the Right from asking the questions? Why was Stacy Abrams not banned after her first loss at Governorship? Why is Hillary Clinton allowed to say she beat Trump, and call him illegitimate? Even the White House Press Secretary was called on her past statements, but never banned. Why censor one side, and one side only? If Biden stacks the SCOTUS, will he use this to his advantage to limit one side even further?

The Disinformation Governance Board (DGB) was an advisory board of the United States Department of Homeland Security (DHS), announced on April 27, 2022. The board's stated function is to protect national security by disseminating guidance to DHS agencies on combating misinformation, misinformation, and disinformation that threatens the security of the homeland. Specific problem areas mentioned by the DHS include false information propagated by human smugglers encouraging migrants to surge to the Mexico–United States border, as well as Russian-state disinformation on election interference and the 2022 Russian invasion of Ukraine.[1][2][3]

On May 18, the board and its working groups were "paused" pending review, and board head Nina Jankowicz resigned, as a result of public backlash, mostly from the political right, although criticism also came from progressives and civil libertarians.[3][4][5][6] On August 24, 2022, Department of Homeland Security Secretary Alejandro Mayorkas disbanded the board.[7]

https://en.wikipedia.org/wiki/Disinformation_Governance_Board

Biden did try his hand at setting up an ill conceived, and poorly administrated board that would oversee information shared, and report it back to the Biden administration. If that doesn't scare people on both sides of the aisle, it should. What you share about the 2020 election is already banned and silenced, so what else do they want to control? Mayorkas should be focusing on the southern border, where he has more troubles than he will ever face in this world again. He doesn't need to focus on anything else at the moment. Nina Jankowicz singing Mary Poppins tunes with her own take on the Right-Wing citizens was not helpful, AT ALL!! While it was catchy, and in good tune, just not appropriate. Maybe she missed her calling, singing is definitely not something she is bad at. A Biden stacked SCOTUS, and a newly revamped Disinformation Governance Board will not bode well for American's, well certain American's. And I don't think that having conversations, about anything is something the Homeland Security needs to be involved in.

There seems to be a theme with the list I put together, they are almost all controversial. There is a huge push by the Left to introduce subject matter, and at early ages. Kindergarten through Grade Three seems to be where many on the Left want to start educating children on gender issues. Revamping the education system to include Critical Race Theory, gender assignment, sexual preference, or any other similar teachings would distract children. Kindergarten children need to learn how to count, play with others, tell time, learn to listen, be kind to others, and how to share. Once they learn these lessons, they will be able to deal with heavier subject matter like gender, race, sex, and so on. Parents and teachers need to be on the same page. I will take this opportunity to say that I believe my education process was made so enjoyable because of the amazing teachers my little country school had growing up. Mountain View Public School in Goulais River was a great place to learn. It was filled with teachers, and a great Principal that always put the student's first. This was something I came to understand more and more as I aged. If I compared those teachers to the teachers, I had in Highschool, I would say they were more hands on. My Highschool teachers didn't care for us less, they had a job to do to get us ready for college, or University. I feel that changing the subject matter would take away from future student's receiving the same experiences as mine. Kid's need to learn math, reading, writing, printing, telling time, colours, etc. Parent's have always been a huge part of their kid's education. I remember my classmates' parents fondly from parent/teacher nights. And I still remember parent night at our Highschool, when we started in Grade 9, in Canada we do K – 8, then Grade 9 – 13 at Highschool. These parents were some of the most caring people I have ever met, and some like my own father have passed on to a reward saved for people just like them. Parents are not domestic terrorists for being invested in their children's education, and what those children receive as an education should always be of the utmost importance. U.S. Attorney General Merrick Garland said that some forms of violence towards school officials could be the equivalent to domestic violence. I am not defending any form of violence, but when you take the parent's concerns out of the equation, place books in school libraries that are pornographic in nature, change curriculum subjects, and have teachers teach children subjects without parental say you get angry parents. In one such case a kindergarten teacher decided to teach her class about gender, having an older student start the lesson with them, then halfway through go change and come back as a different gender, it sparked major pushback. Children were crying, and parents were furious. The teacher knew it would not be something parents would agree upon, so that teacher decided for them what would be best for their children. It was not the right decision, and it was something that would make me incredibly angry if tried by my children's teachers. Can the SCOTUS rule on what our children receive as an education? I am not against truth, nor am I against what is happening in the world around us today. But our youngest children should be allowed to just start school under the regular subject matter, it's so much for them to start to take in to begin with. Let them be children, it goes by so fast as it is.

The subject of gender opens up such a new concept for so many people in the world today. When I was growing up, we didn't, "identify as", we just were. Today you can offend others by calling them the wrong pronoun. In Canada, under Justin Trudeau, and his Liberal Government, words have for the first time been legislated, and prohibited. Unbelievable as it is, I see that becoming more of a thing in the USA as well. If I see a man dressed as a woman, I assume they identify as a woman, why else would they be dressed that way. Likewise, if I see a woman dressed as a man, you get the idea. What I don't understand is the alternate pronouns, the use of, "they", or many others like, "zie". How on earth would I know to call you by that pronoun, if I never knew it existed, or what it even means? Biden's Assistant Secretary of Health Rachel Levine has stated she believes that puberty blockers, and gender affirming care for transgender minors is crucial. My biggest concern here is the shear number of people who have regretted any kind of permanent gender change, and the inability to simply stop taking gender reassignment drugs and transition back. And when you allow small children to make decisions that will affect their future, it becomes even more scary. Can a child take their parents to court to allow them this right? Do the courts have the right to tell parents what is best for their children? I am staggered by the confliction of what is the right choice. How difficult this must be for everyone involved. Calling it gender dysphoria, and making people feel like they are mentally broken will never help anyone but allowing children to decide such a thing isn't right either. Parent's will make the best decision they can for their child, that we must trust in, not the court.

Gender has taken over so much of our daily lives that it is more important to people than the economy. In the midterm elections of 2022, many social aspects were what people felt more compelled to vote towards. Democrat candidates were viewed as more accepting towards gender issues, and therefore the red wave that some thought was coming, didn't show up. Which is good like I have already wrote previously, as Biden would just use a Republican majority in both House and Senate as the scapegoat for his continued failures.

The raid on Mar-A-Lago was a poorly planned and executed raid on former President Trump's home. It was to retrieve documents that were already known to be there. Clearly, a judge had to have issued a warrant for a search, and it was a first in US history. What became of it? What did they do with what they found? Were documents classified, or were documents made re-classified? If they were re-classified by a President that came into power after Trump, and changed the status of those documents, should that be allowed? Is that what happened? Well, we don't really know what happened because after the midterm election of 2022, and Biden remained in control of the Senate, it's like it never happened. Was it a campaign tactic?

Ketanji Onyika Brown Jackson was nominated to the SCOTUS by Joe Biden. And during her nomination hearings she was asked to define a woman. Her answer was that she was not a biologist. As a court judge, should she not be able to define what is male and female? Do you really have to be educated to decipher between the sexes? To me, her putting a "woke' issue before what the law states as a woman is problematic. The law clearly outlines what the definition of a woman is, and such those of the court must abide by that definition.

When Judge Brett Kavanaugh was nominated, he was immediately the subject of a sexual scandal. He faced harsh questioning from those sitting on a joint committee. Was he treated fairly by both sides I have already said my peace about that. The Democrats came from a perspective of already guilty in my opinion, and their questions reflected that stance.

When Amy Coney Barrett was nominated and faced questioning, she was scrutinized heavily as well by Democrat questions. My favourite part was when she was answering multiple questions based on law, and when she was asked to show her notes, she was using to answer, she held up a blank pad of paper. She knew what she was talking about without the use of notes, which really should have confirmed her nomination as justified. Her questions were difficult, and she was asked by VP Harris about personal feelings, which is funny when Barrett answered saying that is not how a judge should arrive at a decision. Then fast-forward to Judge Brown and she can't answer what a woman is, based on her personal view.

It leads me to ask two final questions before moving on from the SCOTUS. Should the highest court in the land, not be made to follow what the law clearly sets out as definition, above that of wokeness? With the Democrats thinking about stacking the SCOTUS, is there a reason to worry about the answer to the first question?

Chapter Twenty-One –

Social Media

For the last number of years, the social media platform has been owned and controlled by those supporting the Democrat Party. They have silenced and censored numerous posts by those of the Right-Wing support. So, being able to shut down, and remove, or control what people opposed to your own viewpoint share is a huge advantage to your side. With social media being the number one place people turn to get their news today, and that includes political news, control of this platform is crucial. Having a strong social media presence during elections is becoming more important that signs in the ground around town. With more people engaged using social media, than person to person, hiring a team to manage, and create your online presence has become very important.

Enter Elon Musk to the ownership of Twitter, and things have now changed slightly for the better. Many on the Left are saying they are leaving the platform, and that things have gotten out of control. One case a certain celebrity started to pretend to be Elon Musk and was tweeting as if she were. It got that person banned and the Left is using that ban as one reason things are out of hand. What did she think would happen? Why would she think it would be alright to do such a thing? Well, suck it up because people on the Right have been banned for years now, and over far less than pretending to be the owner of the platform. The Left has enjoyed being able to say

anything without regard, or fact checking, and are now getting a small taste of reality.

Let's look at some things the Left has gotten away with.

1. Elisabeth Warren – 0 taxes, Musk's ego, Native American

2. Disinformation Governance Board

3. Russia, Iran, but no Trump

4. Free speech for Left.

5. 2020 election

6. Left election denial of 2016/ Abrams ok.

These are obviously just a few things that came to mind, and there are a whole lot more. Elisabeth Warren was again fact checked for tweeting that Biden has the official right and power to cancel student debt, and she was fact checked with plenty of information regarding this, and how it was struck down by a federal court.

Let's start by just looking at the examples I listed above, and that will prove my point. When Twitter was not owned by Musk, those on the Left were allowed to say anything without regard to factually being correct. Elisabeth Warren is a great place to start as she has stated that Elon Musk paid zero in taxes, and that he is free loading off others. While she was so busy telling people that and not being fact checked, Elon Musk has paid the most by a single person in US history paying $11B in taxes. Imagine not being corrected for such a statement about the one person who has paid the absolute most, ever.

Now Elisabeth Warren is no stranger to stretching the truth. Her claim of Native American ancestry, and the use of this on her bar license, and countless town halls, speeches, etc. showcases that she is willing to exaggerate. Her Native American ancestry makes up less than 1/1024, which means if she is 1% Irish, she is way more Irish than she is Native American, but she only identifies as the latter.

Does it really matter if she says she is Native? No, it just calls into question her honesty, as an adult we stop playing pretend long time ago, and people need to speak in truths. Now she is Native American, 1/1024, so she isn't making a false claim, but she should stop saying and using it on her bar license. Whatever gives you an edge I guess, use it.

Warren has a clear anger issue with Musk, and his taking over of one of the social media platforms takes away from the Left having a huge advantage over the Right. It also takes away from the Left namely Warren making claims without fact checking. I can see why she is angry, after having it so good, for so long, but then having to come back to reality, it would be hard.

The short-lived Disinformation Governance Board was another great way of censoring the Right and using the guise of Homeland Security risks as the reason to shut down conversation between the Right and their supporters, didn't go over well. First of all, it looked more like Biden was trying to shut down one side, because his side was still enjoying a monopoly on social media. Secondly, it was ill conceived, and poorly timed. I also feel it looks very similar to antics used by Germany back in WWII to keep people informed on only those things the government feels you should know. I am sure we have not seen the last of this board and would not be surprised it comes back in full swing just before the next Presidential election in 2024. Best way to gain the advantage is to limit what the opposition can talk about, or share.

This is ironic that the Biden team has decided to launch a board to really control disinformation. Coming from a man who himself has said when he took office there was no vaccine. The very vaccine that he had two shots of before being sworn into office. And has made claims that by spending so much money that the USA is suffering from a 40 year high in inflation but has somehow cut the debt in half. That is incredible, how on earth could that even be remotely true. Well, the DGB would have been all over that statement, if it was from a Right-Wing person. Biden is not worried about false claims, or disinformation being shared from his side, and obviously whatever the Democrats are saying is of zero concern to the Homeland Security ears. State run propaganda is what I think of whenever I hear Disinformation Governance Board.

Social media is not the best place to gather your news sources from. There is no real accounting for what people share. People like to create funny memes, and share made up facts to get reactions from people. We have what people call trolls, who love to just piss others off for the fun of it. So, if this is where you are getting your news from, you should be careful and research it further. The really glaring problem with social media is who can use it, and who is not allowed. Russia has invaded Ukraine twice in the last three Presidents. Obama and Biden, affecting millions of lives, destroying livelihoods, and homes, and families. Yet, they have not been banned from the use of any platform. And therefore, can freely share information with others about their views, or what is happening, and why.

Not only is Russia allowed to share their views, but Iran is allowed to share their views about the Jewish State, and its residents. Their view of the Jewish people is not an overwhelmingly warm view. And yet, they continue to be able to share this view. Donald Trump is not allowed as a former President, not allowed to use social media. His first term in office was one of the most successful of any first terms, and yet he is banned. The Democrats claimed and investigated him for a possible collusion with Russia, then they impeached him on a phone call, then they blamed him for shutting down the border for Covid19, then they blamed him for the numbers going high because they wanted him to shut things down. Then they impeached him for January 6th Capital riots. They raided his home for documents they knew were there and had already been allowed to come and see. Yet there have been zero charges, or anything other than a media bashing come of it all. He has announced his running for President in the 2024 election as of November 2022 but is banned from using social media. If he runs again and wins, will the Democrats working alongside the media go back to constant negative coverage, impeachment attempts, and similar bans? You can count on it!!!

What this ban means is free speech is only enjoyed by one side. And if you find yourself on the opposite side of the political views held by the people running social media platforms, you can believe your personal say will be watched, and silenced if necessary. My video talking about what I believe happened on election night 2020 was taken down by YouTube, and most of the things I talked about have come true. So, if we are not allowed to voice an opinion, and showcase that opinion with what we believe to be proof of why we hold that opinion, is that violating our free speech? Yes, the answer is yes. If other countries can proclaim hatred towards a group of people, and if the Democrats can proclaim things that are not true, why can't a person discuss the election integrity? When Bernie Sanders goes on television late night talk shows, and discusses the exact result, involving the exact States, and the surprise result, naturally people would consider this odd. Especially when Bernie did it four days before it happened and was exact with his predictions. I'm not saying that anything did happen that could be linked to cheating, but shouldn't people be allowed to discuss it? And if no one is allowed to talk about it, doesn't that make it seem more like someone is hiding something? After the 9/11 attacks people had opinions, and conspiracy theories, to this day people talk about that. No one shut down the conversations, no one was banned. But Donald Trump and anyone that mentions election integrity gets silenced.

The 2020 election should not be off limits to anyone to talk about. If the Democrats like Stacy Abrams can claim she didn't lose to Kemp in Georgia, and Hillary didn't lose to Trump in 2016, why then is the 2020 election the only election that can't be talked about, or claims of integrity questioned? Just one single election, out of how many elections across the United States, but one single election gets videos, and posts removed, and silenced by the Left, and their supporters. My views of the 2020 election are not important, but what is important is the right for people to freely talk about things. By making one single election off limits to discuss, more concerns arise from what could possibly be the reason. Especially since the side that is doing the ban has openly refused to admit defeat and has stated that elections have been stolen from them.

I will be the first person to say I love using social media. I also love to debate my views on all kinds of subjects. Being told that I can not discuss a topic, but others have stated the same things as people wanting to discuss the 2020 election only makes me want to discuss it more. I don't really have anything I want to say about the 2020 election, but I should have the right to say something if I did. I defend free speech.

Donald Trump running again for President in 2024 will have a very difficult time getting a positive message out on social media. With this platform having such a huge impact on people's lives, and people relying on social media more and more, Trump will be at a disadvantage. Unless Twitter evens the playing field now that Elon Musk is in charge. The importance of social media is abundantly clear when you think about Musk paid $44B or so for the online platform. Jeff Bezos was applauded for his purchase of the Washington Post, and Zuckerberg owning both Facebook and Instagram are not problematic to anyone, but Elon Musk who seems to be a Republican supporter has received backlash for purchasing Twitter.

Whatever your personal viewpoint is politically, or your viewpoint of other people, you should only be silenced if you are being hateful. Hate has no place in our world, and certainly should not be allowed to be shared and posted on the internet. Freedom of speech is a huge right we should all be allowed to share. Conspiracy theories are more fun, and entertaining than they are a worry to the Homeland Security, and 99% are just harmless debate among friends. The use of social media has allowed people to stay connected that might be far away from each other, and during trips. The incredible ability to share in other's lives is what makes the platform so enjoyable. It was created to bring people together in a way, which is what the

United States needs more of, not less. More division, and separation only gives way to animosity, and hate. And using the platform to mislead people on purpose because you can, without accountability is shameful, and wrong. People who feel they have to leave any platform because they don't like to hear opposing ideas, feel free to leave then, but that is not a healthy way to go through life. Echo chambers are not healthy dwellings.

Chapter Twenty-Two –

Chasing Chaos

With the trends we have witnessed from the Left lately, there is no signs of returning from the path they are on. There is no unity in the near future if the two paths are running in different directions. Biden talked about unity in past speeches, but has not helped cultivate it in his actions, or his use of executive order to pass things that would not pass in the Senate and House. Spending absurd amounts of money, increasing inflation, and debt that future generations will have to bear the burden for is wrong. Blaming 40-year high inflation on the fact Russia invading Ukraine also makes no sense. Depending on other countries to help America's fossil fuel needs, but canceling any production to help yourself, is not the right way to go. Releasing reserve barrels of oil to try and reduce the skyrocketing cost of buying foreign oil, only leaves America in worse shape if there is a war, or emergency. With absolutely no effect on the cost in the end.

Educating our children should not be driven by woke ideologies and should not be something that will confuse more than educate. Eroding the innocence of children will not make them better decision makers in the future. It will not create anything other than confusion, but in a world chasing chaos, what else could we imagine. Children need to learn how to count, read, write, and interact. Not learning how to judge each other based on any multitude of reasons, while accusing others of awful things if they differ. Come to think of it, adults need to stay away from that as well.

I do not believe we have totally given up on unity, but it is the farthest away it has ever been. Trump did not create this divide; he has been out of office and things have gotten ridiculously worse since he has. Will a potential second time in office make things better? I would have to say what Trump's administration accomplished in his four years was much better than what Biden has done in two years. So many of Biden's decisions have brought about negative reactions.

1. Student debt payoff
2. No pipelines/drilling
3. Border wall cancellation
4. Weak international policy, (Afghanistan pullout, Ukraine, China)
5. Education (woke agenda, parents viewed as threats)
6. Censorship
7. Defund police.
8. Weak on crime stance
9. Misinformation passed as fact.
10. Gender affirming health care for minors.

These things that Biden is working on haven't helped the country. One could ask, "are we better off today than we were two years ago?" The answer to that question is a very clear NO. Why you ask? Well, because we are chasing the wrong things. What should we be doing?

Well, the country needs to start going after things that strengthen the country. Instead of saying that interest in the economy is similar to what the Nazi Party was interested in. Yes, people on the Left actually said this. The economy is what will get rid of the inflation that Biden created. So, what should the USA be focused on?

1. Economy
2. Education (getting back to a regular curriculum)

3. The border

4. Election integrity

5. Energy independence

6. Unity

7. Mental health

8. Free speech

The Democrats along with the Left are creating an environment where they are trying to change the moral fiber of society. Telling people to defund, and to not trust the police. AOC herself said during the January 6th capital riot that she was afraid of the police officer in her hallway. They are trying to make old fashioned values something to be scrutinized for. Riots are mostly peaceful, criminals need to be released, bail is racist, immigration is not needed, open borders are secure ones, voting is for anyone, and identification is not needed. Acts of violence towards police has risen incredibly, crime is skyrocketing, and spending on Democrat social ideology has caused a 40yr high in inflation. The Democrats have created an America that is justifying the double standard. Where the media covers for their short falls, and where teenage children wearing MAGA hats are targeted without cause. They want people to be at odds with each other. They want their side to attack and cancel the opposition, so they have an advantage. They don't want unity, because unity means accountability, and chaos is easier to control when you are causing it in the first place.

America is in need of change, that we can all agree upon. What needs to change, well that's where we disagree. Half the country wants to go back to the way things were a few years ago, when we could disagree without having people canceled, or fired. When you could debate an issue, talk about it without being labelled as some form of hate monger. The other half wants to chase chaos, and every time they catch it, someone pays the price.